Lorenzo Sears

The Occasional Address

Its Composition and Literature

Lorenzo Sears

The Occasional Address
Its Composition and Literature

ISBN/EAN: 9783337205058

Printed in Europe, USA, Canada, Australia, Japan

Cover: Foto ©ninafisch / pixelio.de

More available books at **www.hansebooks.com**

THE
OCCASIONAL ADDRESS

ITS COMPOSITION AND LITERATURE

BY

LORENZO SEARS, L.H.D.

Professor in Brown University.   Author of " The History of
Oratory from the Age of Pericles to the Present Time "

G. P. PUTNAM'S SONS
NEW YORK & LONDON
THE KNICKERBOCKER PRESS
1897

To

My Classmate

HON. SIMEON E. BALDWIN, LL.D.

Professor of Constitutional and Mercantile Law

in

Yale University

PREFACE.

THE design of the following chapters is to present the main requirements for the production of the Occasional Address. A consideration of its principal elements of structure is followed by an examination of the forms which it has assumed, thus making possible both the synthetic and the analytic treatment of the subject. In preparing the work I have borne in mind chiefly the needs of students who may be interested in the basis and structure of oratorical composition. Still, I believe that serviceable suggestions may be found by professional speakers for the extra-professional tasks which they are often asked to perform. Some assistance also may be afforded to a considerable number in every vocation, who are from time to time called upon to give effective presentation of their thoughts in public speech.

Occasions for addresses of various kinds are constantly recurring under the present conditions of American life. The ordinary responsibilities of citizenship impose the frequent necessity of recalling and interpreting lessons taught by memorable events and illustrious lives, and of impressing upon the public serious views and recommendations concerning matters of pending policy. Opportunities are also frequently offered to contribute to the entertainment of the hour by a few gracefully spoken words.

Such occasions in the past have evoked a literature corresponding to their diversified character. Reference has been made to the greater part of this literature in the hope that it will be found full of suggestion to those who may be called upon to meet the demands of similar occasions in the future.

L. S.

Brown University,
February, 1897.

CONTENTS.

PART I.

ELEMENTS OF STRUCTURE.

CHAPTER I.—INTRODUCTORY.

PAGES

CHAPTER II.—THE OBJECT OF DISCOURSE.

CHAPTER III.—THE SUBJECT.

vii

CHAPTER IV.—THE PLAN.

CHAPTER V.—THE INTRODUCTION.

CHAPTER VI.—THE DISCUSSION.

CHAPTER VII.—THE CONCLUSION OF AN ADDRESS.

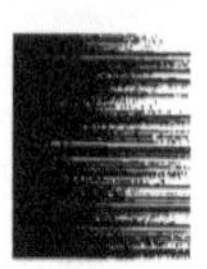

Contents ix

PART II.

QUALITIES OF EXPRESSION.

CHAPTER I.—CARDINAL PROCESSES.

CHAPTER II.—PERSPICUITY.

CHAPTER III.—ENERGY.

CHAPTER IV.—ELEGANCE.

Chapter V.—Adaptation.

Chapter VI.—Personal and Ethical Qualities.

PART III.

FORMS OF OCCASIONAL ADDRESS.

Chapter I.—The Eulogy.

Contents xi

Contents

" Do you think that you could speak yourself if there were
a necessity, and if the council were to choose you ?

"And what would you be able to say if you had to speak ?"

The Menexenus of Plato.

(JOWETT'S VERSION.)

PART I.

ELEMENTS OF STRUCTURE.

I.

INTRODUCTORY.

THE comprehensive term, Occasional Address, is here employed to designate those forms of public speech which are called forth by occurrences of unusual importance. It is a custom in our own **Definition.** time and nation, as it has been in other nations and times, to interpret in this manner the meaning of events, to recall the teaching of turning-points in history, to commemorate worthy lives, and to enforce the lessons exemplified in noble characters. As a custom, it has its reason and justification, partly in the reminiscent disposition common to all people, and also in the willingness and desire to be guided in the larger affairs of personal and national life by the wisdom which is distilled from the experience of the past. Thus the occasional ad-

3

dress has grown to be a feature in the life and literature of all cultivated nations.

In our own nation in particular it has become prominent, owing to a strong inclination to celebrate anniversary days and, as a republic, to keep in constant remembrance the lessons of political wisdom left by its founders. The better sentiment of the people is, that the continuance of our institutions depends upon an educated public understanding and conscience. Among the instrumentalities for accomplishing this,—such as the establishing of societies of a commemorative character, and the increasing study of our history, and the preservation of memorials, —must be reckoned the occasional address in one or more of its forms. Indeed, it usually accompanies the above-mentioned retrospective acts; for the foundation or mere continuance of any organization or ceremony avails little unless occasionally explained and illustrated. The spoken word of comment, instruction, and appeal must pass between the event and the common intelligence or its best significance and its power are ultimately lost.

Interpreted rightly, the event, life, or character obtains a widely radiating influence, a renown commensurate with its exposition, and a usefulness as varied as the diversified views of different interpreters.

The value of such occasional address may best be estimated by recalling some example of it. One need go no farther back than the centennial of Washington's inauguration as President of the United States. *Its value.* The years since have been prolific in such discourse. Every intelligent citizen will remember what some instance of it has been to him when he has had set before him higher ideals of citizenship or nobler standards of character than those presented in the ordinary round of daily living. Perchance, the historic spirit may have been stirred and the historic imagination fired—no inferior elements in the education of a man who has other interests than those of finance. Possibly the theme may have been merely literary, scientific, or social in character; the departments of taste, knowledge, and good fellowship occupy too large a portion of what is called life to permit the neglect of any method of cultivation so effective as the popular lecture in its earlier or later forms.

It may be said that the teachings above mentioned can be had from other sources; those of justice, for example, in the courts, of the higher politics in legislative assemblies, and of morals and religion in the pulpit. But these specialties are each subject to qualifications as methods of instruction, and their limitations are so obvious as to be an answer to the suggestion to substitute them for the public address as popular educators. Such instruction is in definite lines, often technical, or restricted to narrow bounds by necessity, taste, habit, and class association. Topics that can be discussed before a representative throng of the people are out of place in any and all the departments of instruction just enumerated. Both the audience and the address are more general in character. The one will have a wider scope, and the other will be composed of more heterogeneous materials. On the other hand, the hearers expect to be instructed in matters of superior interest and importance, or to have

Compared with other oratorical forms.

inspiring examples set before them, their best motives appealed to, and to hear all in a dignified and elevated tone of discourse.

For this they naturally look to their leaders —men of intelligence, wisdom, and effective speech. As a rule, these are men of education and cultivation. Usually they belong to the constantly widening circle of the learned professions. As these are becoming more learned and more technical with the growth of specialism, the chances for the best occasional oratory are growing less. The qualities which make men eminent at the bar, in the legislature, in the pulpit, the editorial office, the academic lecture-room, must converge at one point where each man shall be a recognized authority according to his eminence. He may be an occasional orator, but the occasions will be as rare as the demand is infrequent for what he can say best.

Accordingly there is the greater demand upon professional and educated men to cultivate those faculties which will be of service in extra-professional address, and to make excursions into those fields of knowledge which lie outside their narrowing vocations. For in this territory the great multitude of men live and move, with their interests and hopes and fears, their ignorance and their shrewd sense, their fickleness and their power, their prejudices and their openness to conviction and persuasion. To nothing are they more obedient than to the skilled speaker who knows whereof he speaks. As intelligence increases and becomes the condition of privilege and power, and even of liberty, the people will come in greater numbers to hear what the man will say whose knowledge and virtue give him the right to address them. They will listen and pay him their best tribute in adopting his opinions, and possibly in repeating them as their own on the first opportunity. They may not understand all that he says; they may recall still less after his speech is ended, but they have received information, impressions, and impulses through the words spoken, and, what is often of equal value, through the speaker's personality and character, evident to the discerning spirit in every audience.

Nothing is better adapted to give a speaker the power needed to inform and direct multitudes, than a study of the occasional address both in its structure and as a literary form. In the first respect, it has much in common with other kinds of oratory, as the judicial, the deliberative, and the homiletic. Still, this fourth form, the demonstrative, emphasizes certain methods which give it distinction from the others. Above all it is what the Greeks called " epidictic "—showing forth—and the Romans, " demonstrative," not in the sense of demonstration by logical processes so much as by expository setting forth and pointing out, as of a thing in itself plain when attention has been directed to it. If this demonstration or exhibition and display of truth is made for the purpose of securing a definite act on the part of those addressed, the discourse becomes " determinative," as directing to a certain end. The same term applies to that address which is intended to result in a change of opinion, belief, or action. In such discourse there is need of clear perception and the power to make evident to others what is seen by the speaker. In technical phrase, the speaker should have the qualities of perspicacity and perspicuity ; be keen of sight, and plain in speech. So only will he be both a discoverer and a revealer. He will also need in their place and time other subordinate qualities which are commonly set down in works upon composition, and cannot safely be omitted in any treatment of methods in the expression of thought. But the widest exposition of effective processes and qualities in occasional oratory is found in its literature, which is abundant and diversified.

Every nation and century have contributed to it according to their character, taste, and ability. The Greek gave it a nobly reminiscent and commemorative tone, the Roman a panegyric accent ; the mediæval ecclesiastic emphasized the spirit of reverence ; the French orators breathed into it a loyalty to imperialism mingled with an unswerving devotion to the King of kings ; the English made it a moderate and just estimate of events and men ; while Americans, the heirs of all, have given it a cosmopolitan character and a

free treatment. The entire body of this literature in all nations and times is the best of instructors to any who may have to speak in a
similar strain. Its volume is great, but the
choicest of it is accessible and sufficient. Full
of instruction, suggestion, and inspiration in its
matter, and of dignity and beauty in its form,
replete with graces of style, the strength of
clear presentation, and the force of sympathetic
appeal, it is a type of the most effective communication, from one man to many, of his per-
ceptions and opinions, his sentiments and
emotions. What the masters of such speech
accomplished in the determinative mode of it,
belongs to the history of eloquence and of
civilization itself. Therefore any study of demonstrative oratory should, as far as practicable, include reference, at least, to its literature.
Extended quotation in any work of moderate
compass is impossible, as it is also misleading
if fragmentary. Only as illustrating separate
divisions of discourse can the discourse itself
be divided without marring the effect of its unity
and completeness. Accordingly, while sources
of instruction and suggestion have been indi-

cated here, so much only of extract and analysis has been made as will lead to the synthesis of actual composition. The two processes together constitute the method which contributes to best success in this important phase of public speech.

Before undertaking an occasional address there will, of course, arise questions as to the orator's reason for speaking at all, the object and purpose he has in mind, the end he desires to accomplish, and his own warrant for the attempt. These interrogatories being answered, matters of construction will demand attention, in the main divisions of introduction, discussion, and conclusion. Qualities which make for effectiveness in presenting thoughts and appealing to motives cannot be overlooked, nor, above all, certain impalpable elements which are gifts rather than acquirements, the greatest of which is the moral strength and earnestness that underlie the most effective speech. In demonstrative discourse, more than in any other form, there is a demand for all these and every other resource of oratory, since those who are addressed belong to every grade in the social scale, and hold opinions, sentiments, and beliefs of endless diversity.

Consequently the study of the occasional address as composition is widely inclusive, as its literature is almost limitless. The following chapters attempt to apply familiar principles and methods to this single branch of discourse, and also to point out its achievements in several directions, ranging from sober commemoration to the lighter speech of social festivities. If, in consequence of this attempt, it shall be easier to keep the occasional address up to the high levels which it has reached in our own and in former times, the purpose of this discussion of its composition and its literature will be accomplished.

Treatment of subject outlined.

II.

THE OBJECT OF DISCOURSE.

IT has been observed that the literature of the Anglo-Saxon race has for one of its fundamental characteristics a definite purpose, which in turn becomes the reason of its exist-

Object in speaking. ence and the warrant of its perpe-tuity. In some forms of composition this element of purpose will necessarily not be avowed, although even in a novel it is not needful to assent to a recent critical dictum that " a story with a purpose is a violation of the author's unwritten contract with his read-ers." The announcement of the writer's pur-pose is, however, by no means essential. On the contrary, such proclamation of the speak-er's design may be the most direct and speedy means of frustrating it, as the premature publi-cation of a warrant for arrest puts the offender

14

on guard and hastens his escape. So far as the audience is concerned, the purpose of a discourse is sometimes subject to the same law that prevails in the novel or the play, where it would be fatal to the reader's prolonged attention to state, as in the ancient prologue, the purpose of the story or the drama. But in the degree that the speaker is at variance with his hearers, it will be politic to keep his intention to himself. The last thing they will wish to hear is, that he purposes to change their way of thinking, and bring them around to a contrary opinion. Consistency is a jewel which every man thinks he possesses, and with which he never parts. Accordingly the skilled orator does not publicly propose to change the opinions of his audience. In proportion as he really desires to accomplish this he will avoid proclaiming his design.

In just this proportion also, on the other hand, will his object in speaking be clear and definite to himself. This purpose must be the first and clearest thought that he Purpose clear has. It is not to be denied that to himself. there are felicitous speakers to whom sympathetic assemblies listen with pleasure when there is nothing of great consequence to hear; but the manner in which the little or nothing is said gives pleasure for the time, and in this way becomes the purpose of the hour to the spokesman. At such a time a serious purpose might be as much out of place as a sermon at a marriage feast. Yet the purpose of the speech in lighter vein may be just as definite and just as apposite as when graver issues are discussed with the definite aim to win opposing minds to the speaker's own. When, however, serious matters press upon the orator, he will realize the strong necessity of having the purpose of his discourse clearly and definitely in mind. For the very nature of persuasive speech implies an object and end for which it is uttered. Not mainly to instruct, like the essay or the lecture, nor chiefly to please, like the story, the poem, and the play; but being designed to move the sentiments toward a higher plane, or the wills of the hearers to determinate action, the end to which such speech is directed must be the plainest, clearest, and earliest thought in the writer's mind. Otherwise his effort will be divided, vague, and uncertain, with corresponding results. In nothing is singleness of aim more essential to success, or division and indistinctness more fatal. Incidentally it may be remarked here that the objects of speaking may in general be reduced to four: to enlighten the understanding, to please the imagination, to move the passions, and to influence the will. Eloquence itself, in the large significance of the word, denotes " that art or talent by which discourse is adapted to its purpose."

The first inquiry, therefore, which the orator makes will be, What is the object of my speech? What, indeed, is the reason of my speaking at all? This question is **Purpose in different kinds of discourse.** pertinent whatever may be the nature of the discourse. If forensic, the character of the case will furnish the answer, whether prosecution or defence. If deliberative, the measure to be advocated. If political, the end to be gained. If commemorative, the lesson to be inculcated. If inaugural, inceptive, or anticipatory, the promise, the hope, and the expectation will furnish the speaker with a purpose to lead his hearers up to the efforts they

are to make to meet incident obligations.   A
lecture has its instruction to be conveyed, and
a sermon both instruction and persuasion.

The literature of eloquence affords many examples of such inquiry, which must have been
made by orators before their speeches
Examples.
were begun, or even planned.   To
cite an instance which will be recalled by every
reader of such literature: In the Bunker Hill
oration by Daniel Webster, at the laying of the
corner-stone of the monument, his preconceived
purpose was plainly to show the results of the
Revolutionary war upon civilization, and to
urge the people to perpetuate the existing condition of prosperity.   Charles Summer's object
in his oration on " Fame and Glory," delivered
before the literary societies of Amherst College
in August, 1847, was to establish a higher ideal
in the moral life, to emphasize the brotherhood
of mankind, and to bring human lives into
harmony with the divine will.   The object of
Wendell Phillips's " Phi Beta Kappa" oration at
Harvard, June 30, 1881, was to show that man
with a college education may educate and ele-
vate the masses.   The purpose of William H.

Seward's speech on "The Irrepressible Conflict,"
1858, was to encourage the people of the United
States in reclaiming ground which had been
surrendered to the interests of the South.
Robert Toombs, of Georgia, had in mind a
purpose to impress the North with the consequences of inconsistency to its former doctrine
of loyalty to the decisions of the Supreme
Court, and to show that secession and an appeal to arms would follow.   Jefferson Davis in
his inaugural address tried to brace the energies
of the Confederacy to the responsibility of con-
ducting its own affairs, and to securing the
perpetuity of the separated government.   Carl
Schurz in 1864 had, as the end and aim of his
Milwaukee speech, the fortifying of the war
sentiment and further sacrifice for the cause of
Union and Liberty. To emphasize the doctrine
that Congress should guarantee republican
government in the Southern States after the
war, was the purpose of Henry Winter Davis's
speech in March, 1864, and Geo. H. Pendle-
ton's reply was for the purpose of recalling the
old doctrine of the rights of States.   In all
these instances, if one were asked what was the

chief thought of each speaker at the outset, the answer would be, "His purpose." An end is to be secured. A certain man desires to accomplish it, and determines to make the attempt. This thought is prior to any definite vision of the precise method by which the object is to be gained. The particular line of address is a later decision. To make a speech will certainly not be the first impulse with a man in earnest; at least not for the sake of speaking. Only as a means to an end will he make a public address; unless he delights in the inebriety which it sometimes produces— especially in extemporaneous effusions—but with corresponding reactions and disgust on the following day, or even earlier. Accordingly, every speaker who is likely to be heard with interest will have a purpose, or find one, as the justification of his appearing before an audience with a demand upon its time and attention. The age is too busy, and the aggregated hours surrendered by listeners are too many to admit of waste on purposeless talk by which time is lost and energies dissipated.

In considering the object and purpose of

speaking, the same exercise of judgment is required as in all the serious affairs of life. Nowhere is the need greater than here, that the speaker rightly estimate his ability to accomplish his ends and satisfy a laudable ambition. In general it may be affirmed, that an overmastering purpose will give earnestness and sincerity to utterance, but unfortunately these qualities, essential as they are to eloquence, are by no means the whole of it. Many a person who has been stirred by a clear vision of the worthiness of some form of beneficence, or by an oppressive sense of a long-standing wrong, has also felt his powerlessness to "cry aloud and spare not." The incubus of compelled silence is upon him. He cannot find his voice. Not all, however, are thus choked by an overwhelming sense of inequality to the occasion and the demand. As a consequence, many causes have been espoused, and many enterprises undertaken, by zealous but miscalculating champions. This is exemplified in every reform movement. There were many, for instance, who were eager to abolish the slave-trade in England and in this country, but only two or three who were able to be leaders in such a stupendous undertaking. Opportunities for a crusade against permitted wrongs are never wanting, nor is the perception of them long absent from keen sensibilities in every community and age; but the able are always fewer than the devoted and the valiant.

It therefore becomes a part of the difficulty and the labor which beset a speaker at the outset to estimate with exactness his aptitude to achieve a desired end. He will ask: "Am I equal to the enterprise I have in mind? Can I reasonably expect to accomplish it? Is my desire a warrant of my success? Can I command the forces requisite to stem opposition, and turn it to my advantage?" Such questions are not so rare or idle as they may seem. Out in the strife of opinions, parties, and factions they are constantly presenting themselves to the men who are guiding public sentiment and enlisting forces. Their success depends largely upon the discreet answers they make to the above self-questionings. Therefore, one lesson to be learned is how to make a wise estimate of what can

safely be undertaken as the object of persuasive speech, in order that the purpose to be
accomplished be not beyond the ability of him
who ardently desires its attainment.

How is this to be ascertained? Sometimes
by nothing less than the actual trial, in which
the speaker may surprise himself and develop
unexpected resources. Usually, however, he
will need some previous encouragement or dissuasion. Then reference to past achievements
may be helpful. Has a similar task been performed with satisfaction? Would a friend of
similar capacity be likely to undertake it or
carry it to a successful conclusion? Has it
been taken up before, and by what sort of
advocates, and with what result? Such in-
quiries will clarify doubts and settle uncertain-
ties. At least they will be likely to indicate
the safe side and may prevent disaster. Or,
possibly, they may lead to a reasonable assur-
ance of success. For example, when Daniel
Webster undertook to reply to Hayne's attack
upon him and upon New England, it is certain
that he had few apprehensions as to his com-
petency to meet the charges of his opponent.

His entire political education had been fitting him for that day's business. He needed but a few hours to gather up the studies of years. Some colleague of his would have felt called upon to take up the gauge of battle if he had not been present to answer for himself and Massachusetts, but with what inadequacy to the occasion and with what disparity in the result ! No such misgiving crossed Webster's mind as he called for the reading of Foote's resolution, and braced himself for a four-hours' discussion of the principles of union under the Constitution. Neither had Charles Sumner any hesitancy as to his ability to discuss the issues involved in the Kansas-Nebraska bill, nor had Wendell Phillips in any exposition of similar themes before incredulous or hostile throngs. One and all knew their strength, and were reasonably sure of carrying out their well-formed plans.

It is easy to record the instances where failures have been made, but their frequency makes them less remarkable than preeminent successes. In general it may be said, other things being equal, that, whenever a speaker has failed, the primary

Dangers of an overestimate.

cause has been an overestimate of his power to accomplish an object which he had in view. He undertook too much, with the usual and proverbial consequence of not counting the cost, and of not measuring his strength. Therefore the orator will not waste the time which he spends in estimating his ability to cope with the obstacles that lie between him and the attainment of his purpose. He will ask if it is within the scope of his ordinary capacity, or at most within the outer circle of his exceptional and extraordinary achievements. Has he a high commission to enter the lists against a gigantic wrong or to defend a just cause, whose advocacy may need still more valor and discretion than the arraignment of an unjust one? Will he, in short, do more harm than good by a weak support, when a strong championship is demanded?

An affirmative answer does by no means compel total silence and entire withdrawal from a good cause. There are many ways of giving it support and many degrees of efficacy in each way; but to render the best service in persuasive speech, much counsel with one's self, and perhaps with others, should be taken, in order to establish that conviction which gives the speaker an assured sense of power and reasonable certainty of success; for these are often of more weight with an audience than what is spoken. Listeners are not slow to discover that the undertaking is greater than the man, that the cause is higher and nobler than the advocate. So likewise they are quick to suspect for what reasons his advocacy has been assumed, whether for the advantage it will bring to him, or for the help he can bring to it. In any case, the orator who hopes to succeed will identify himself with the cause he espouses, entirely and without reserve, so far as it commends itself to him. Otherwise he will abandon it, and devote his energies to something into which he can enter with that single-heartedness which is the chief condition of success. For there are enterprises suited to every man's capacity, as there is some one topic on which almost any intelligent person can speak with confidence in private or in public.

III.

THE SUBJECT.

TO choose a subject is often supposed to be the first step in composing an address. The necessity and the purpose of speaking being established, the topic becomes Choice of subject. the next consideration. " I must speak: what shall I speak about ? " This often brings with itself more difficulty and perplexity than all subsequent questions, for in one sense it includes them all. A world of topics is known to exist, but in the confusion and the obscurity of chaos. Sometimes there are directing agencies coming, perhaps, from an instructor in college, or from the occasion itself, but at the best the opportunity for selection and rejection is large, and much must be left to one's own judgment, with the usual chances of mistake and consequent failure. This must be

charged largely to a neglect of the first question, already considered in the foregoing chapter.   If the object of speaking has been clearly
determined, the choice of a subject will be attended with far less difficulty than if all creation is to be rummaged for something to speak
about.   The purpose being clear, the question
is limited to the most direct method of accomplishing it.   It is simply a matter of the short-
est road to a given point, or the one most
likely to secure the largest following.   The
field is narrowed, a hundred other fields are
excluded, diverging and enticing paths are dis-
missed from consideration, and the general
direction determined.   There is still room left
for variety of treatment, but the course is plain
and, above all, the end of it is fixed.   It is
with the writer as with the preliminary surveyor of a railway route from town to town.
He stands here; he must go yonder; whether
by this mountain and along that stream, or
through this hill and over that hollow—it
makes little difference.   But no questions of
another road in another state, nation, or hemi-
sphere will disturb and distract him.   The

way to take the most people at the least cost
from one place to another is all that concerns
him now. And all that concerns the man who
is to lead others to think as he thinks, to believe as he believes, to do as he does, is to
choose that line of discourse which will bring
them to the point where he stands. This general direction will be indicated by what is
called the subject of discourse. In substance
it includes the entire address, as the acorn includes the oak. It is a seed-truth, or proposition from which all succeeding statements,
expositions, and illustrations grow as naturally
as branches, twigs, and leaves spring from the
trunk of a tree.

In form it is a clause only, according to present standards of taste. Once it was a whole
title-page ; but the discourse was of *Statement of*
proportionate length. When the *subject.*
sermon was measured by the second or third
turning of the hour-glass in New England pul-
pits, how could a single sentence of moderate
length convey an adequate notion of what that
discourse contained? Condensation was not a
Puritan accomplishment. There was too much

time and too large a territory to encourage re-
trenchment. It was two hundred years before
cultivation, discipline, and good taste could
bring the subject of a two-hour oration into
the compass of a single line or clause. "The
True Grandeur of Nations"; "The Character
of Washington"; "Disunion"; "Reconstruc-
tion"; "The War"; "Idols"; "Free Trade";
"The New South,"—all these are examples of
inclusive and comprehensive statement of the
germ idea in as many addresses. Once, the first
thought would have been drawn out as follows:
" New England Persecutors Mauled with their
own Weapons; Giving Some Account of the
bloody laws made at Boston against the King's
Subjects that dissented from their way of Worship. Together with a brief Account of the
Imprisonment and Tryal of Thomas Maule of
Salem for publishing a book entitled, Truth
held forth and maintained, etc. By Theo. Phi-
lolathes." [T. Maule.]

" Boanerges, A Short Essay to preserve and
strengthen the Good Impressions Produced by
Earthquakes on the Minds of People that have
been Awakened with them. Addressed unto

the Whole People of New England who have been Terrified with the late Earthquakes; and more especially the Towns that have had a more singular Share in the Terrors of them." By Cotton Mather, Boston, 1727. Once more by the same: "Memorable Providences, Relating to Witchcrafts and Possessions. A Faithful Account of many Wonderful and Surprising Things, that have befallen several Bewitched and Possessed Persons in New England Particularly. A Narrative of the marvellous Trouble and Releef, Experienced by a pious Family in Boston, very lately and sadly molested by Evil Spirits."

Increase, son of the above, justified his name by the length of the following title: " A Relation of the Troubles which have happened in New England, By reason of the Indians there. From the Year 1614 to 1675. Wherein the frequent Conspiracys of the Indians to cutt off the English and the wonderfull providence of God in disappointing their devices is declared. Together with an Historical Discourse concerning the Prevalency of Prayer; shewing that New England's late deliverance from the Rage of the

Heathen is an eminent Answer of Prayer. By Increase Mather, Teacher of a Church in Boston in New England."

For other and numerous illustrations of early titular expansiveness, the reader is referred to Sabin's *Bibliotheca Americana*, volume xi.

Brevity, however, is not the only quality to be sought under all conditions. If, for instance, the topic of discourse is to be announced beforehand, or to be advertised in any way, there will be sought for it an agreeable statement, euphonic if possible. Publishers of books understand better than authors themselves the value of taking or catching titles. In fiction this is truer than elsewhere, and a book with a rhythm, or a riddle, or a proverb in the title, begins to sell itself, or continues to pass its praise from mouth to mouth. " Murder will Out "; " Love in Idleness "; " Foul Play "; " Hard Cash "; " What will He Do with It ? "; " Looking Backward " ; " Barriers Burned Away "; " Put Yourself in His Place "; " White Lies " ; " Beside the Bonny Briar Bush "; " With Edge Tools "; " Green Pastures and Picadilly,"—all indicate a taste that has prevailed in titles.

To a certain extent this is true of the wording of the subject of any discourse, especially, as has been remarked, when it is to be announced beforehand. Many a preacher or lecturer has depended as much upon startling or enigmatical topics for an attraction as upon what he was considered likely to say. From a single list of "Sunday Announcements" the following samples of subjects are taken: "Excursion from Joppa to Jerusalem"; "Equal Rights a Delusion"; "The Measure of a Man"; "Is He Coming?"; "The Dual Nature of Man"; "Eyes and Ears"; "The Power of Trifles to Annoy"; "Afraid to Join Them." The permanent value of such announcements in a continued series of discourses is not to be discussed here. But that it may be done once with advantage shows that there is something in uniqueness of presentation, which draws a crowd. Continuous attraction will depend more upon the speaker than upon his advertisements.

From these quaint, stilted, and sensational statements of the subject of discourse, atten-

tion may be turned to what is of more consequence to the speaker, namely, the derivation

Derivation of a definite theme from a general
of the theme. topic. He will need to do this for
his own purposes in composition as well as for
the satisfaction of his hearers, in obtaining a
clear understanding of what he has to tell them.
The ordinary process is not beyond the possibility of tracing.

Suppose, in illustration, that the occasion be
academic and anniversary in character. From
the vast departments of human action and
knowledge, suggestions may come flocking to
one who is looking for a subject, and very likely
the most inappropriate and impracticable will
be the first to arrive. Rejection, utter and
absolute, will be the primary process. Con-
sciously or unconsciously, sooner or later, the
writer will find himself so dominated by the
thought of the occasion, that only those topics
which are in harmony with its spirit will be
tolerated for an instant. Themes relating to
education in its narrow or broader meaning will
at last, if not at first, come to the surface in a
form as crude as the reflection " I must speak

upon some educational topic." Then follows the process which is preliminary to a definite statement of the subject of discourse, namely, the determination of the theme. On such a proceeding much time and thought may be profitably expended. In all the wide range covered by such a subject-general as " Education " there are a hundred specific topics that can be discussed and, as every practised writer knows, with greater ease and definiteness than the all-including idea of Education in general. By some such operation of division and subdivision, of rejection and selection, it may be imagined that George William Curtis came to his well-known theme at Union College, " The Public Duty of Educated Men." Education might have suggested to him such topics as Liberal, Technical, Classical, or Scientific Training; for scholars, for business men, for officials, for citizens ; for the few, for the many, at great cost and at little ; in relation to home life and to public affairs. It may have suggested a definite or an indefinite conception, relevant or irrelevant, but none satisfactory, until out of the mass is at length extracted a concrete idea of Education embodied in men who have been educated liberally, coupled with the corporate body of citizens called the State. The obligations of such persons to the aggregated assemblage of all finally finds form in the brief but comprehensive theme, " The Public Duty of Educated Men." A similar procedure brought out of the vast subject of Literature the theme of Edward Everett's first venture in the department of demonstrative oratory—" Circumstances Favorable to the Progress of Literature in America." So, from the general subject of Peace, Charles Sumner drew the lesson that the " True Grandeur of Nations " consists in cultivating and keeping the peace rather than in promoting and practising the arts of war. Slavery in the United States he attacks by a flank movement, when he described the horrors of " White Slavery in the Barbary States."

While therefore the general subject, as in each of these topics, is briefer in its statement than the derived theme, the latter so narrows the idea as to make it easier of treatment. Let any one attempt to write upon Education, Literature, Peace, or Freedom, if he wishes to see how elusive and illusive such vast subjects are. At first sight they appear as grand and fine as a sunset cloud. The first plunge into them reveals nothing but gathering mist. A few generalities about the advantages of Education to the man, and of Peace to a nation, are followed by growing darkness, confusion, and early discouragement. Not until one section of the general subject has been separated from the rest, will there be much satisfactory progress.

This law of division is one of the hardest for the inexperienced writer to understand. To him it seems that the larger and more general the subject, the more there should be to say about it. A book might be written upon Nature, or Art, or Travel, or Genius, or Politics, or Labor, or Character: why not an hour's discourse? The reply might be made that it would be easier to write the book than the discourse: for in a book the subject would be treated section by section, while in the discourse there is usually the attempt to swallow it whole and to make others do the same. The

writer of either form will have to yield to the
unbending law of human infirmity in the matter of apprehension and assimilation. Partial
knowledge, discovery of truth step by step, and
one step at a time, is the rule for the average
understanding, and audience. The speaker
will therefore confine himself to one section of a
subject, or at the extreme to one at a time, for
his own sake, and for the sake of those to whom
he is to speak.

The formal statement of the part of a subject being of necessity longer than that of the
whole, another difficulty arises in
making this statement brief enough

**Comprehens-
ive brevity
in statement.**
for announcement, and at the same
time full enough for adequate comprehension
of the theme. It may not be successfully done
at the start. Beginning with a statement of
some length, a clearer and more compact expression may be gained when the entire composition is finished. Elements which did not
appear at the first outlook may have entered
into the discussion, and some that were first
to show themselves may be like froth that
rises to the seething surface to be cast away.

Rather, however, than not to get a clear and definite idea of what he is going to attempt, the writer had best make the first statement of his theme a page in length, if need be, and trust to his later treatment to clarify, condense, and abbreviate it. An example of a short statement of a subject that might have been long, which in the mind of the orator must at first have been longer than its present form, is Burke's theme, " To the Electors of Bristol." It might have been expanded in the speaker's mind as follows : " The representative of a constituency who is worthy of that constituency and his official position, ought to have some regard to their opinions ; but only to such as are permanent and not shifting, as becomes one who is for the people a pillar of the State, and not a weather vane to show which way the wind of popular whim happens to be blowing at any particular hour." The speech is usually known as that made previous to the Bristol election, but the title might have been : " The Relation of the Representative to his Constituency," or " The Independence of the Representative."

In any stated theme the problem will always

be to incorporate the main, or trunk idea in as few words as will convey its outline

Expression of leading thought. to the audience. Its main features will be enough. More than these belong to the discourse itself. And if these details are stated too fully in the title, so much will be taken from the interest of the speech. As in a novel, there should not be too much anticipatory declaration and revelation giving the plot away too soon. This caution is particularly applicable to those rare occasions when it may be advisable not to indicate the subject too clearly at the outset, or perhaps not at all. In the conflict of opinion and the antagonism of interests it not infrequently happens that prejudices are so strong, and hostility so violent, that when a speaker announces his subject a part, if not the whole, of his audience is at once in opposition. They wish to hear nothing from his side. They do not believe in it and, furthermore, they do not wish to believe in it. To announce, in effect, that the speaker is going to persuade them to his views if he can, is to rouse all their power of resistance, if not to stir up their personal animosity and violence against the speaker himself. Some will leave the room, others will stay to stop the speaking. Such demonstration may be occurring any day, but in the stormy years of the struggle for the Union there were notable examples which have become historic. Sometimes the opposition element was ready to drown a voice which was known to be on the other side, although the subject on which it was to speak had not been announced. Such was the attitude towards Wendell Phillips of the Faneuil Hall mass-meeting, gathered to denounce the murder of Lovejoy, and of a hundred other audiences before which he spoke in the days of pro- and anti-slavery sentiment. Such was the uproarious tumult when George William Curtis was escorted by a bodyguard to a platform in Philadelphia in 1859, and such, once more, was the ruffianly greeting which Henry Ward Beecher received in Liverpool when he essayed to vindicate the North in the Civil War. In all these instances, and others like them, it would be throwing oil on the flame to state the subject which the speaker has most vividly in his own mind. If he must state

it at all it will be when some degree of toler-
ation has been secured ; but the better place is
near the close, when the object and purpose of
the speech is accomplished. Up to this conclusion and end of all persuasion the speaker
has been working his way and drawing his unwilling listeners after him. If he has brought
them to his own point of view at last, it is
soon enough to tell them so, or at least to for-
mulate the wording of a subject which has been
all along definite and clear in his own mind,
and is at length plain to his hearers.

This reservation of the subject, it is to be
borne in mind, is necessary or even justifiable
Reservation   only when an early announcement
of theme.   of it may antagonize an audience.
In all other cases it is to the advantage of
speaker and hearer alike, that the subject be
plainly stated at the beginning of the discourse.
By this it is not meant that the theme is to be
formulated in the opening sentence or even in
the first paragraph. This would savor of a sud-
denness and bluntness which belongs neither to
good art nor to nature, in both of which there are
gradual approaches to any work of dignity and

eminence. Every lofty mountain has its foot-hills; every great river its declining banks, and precipitous surprises are rare. In conversation even, when a person is to be approached on a matter which is uppermost in the speaker's mind, it is kept back until the preparatory commonplaces about the weather or the minister, the crops or the election, business or schools, work or play, shall lead up naturally to the topic of immediate concern. A similar following of nature will be desirable in deliberate address.

IV.

THE PLAN.

THE object of discourse being clear, the theme being definitely stated for one's self, and concisely worded for the hearers, the natural impulse is to begin at once with what is

Value of a plan. to be said. This, however, does not mean taking up the pen to write the first sentence, or even the introductory paragraphs. It might be said that it would be very natural for an orator to proceed at once to what first occurs to him, following this with the next thought, and so on to the end. But, unfortunately, the best oratory is not meditation, rumination, or monologue. Instead, it is organized, methodically arranged thought, having a purpose to accomplish by the most effective disposition of mental forces and verbal expression. As much skill may be required to determine the order and sequence of thoughts, or even of words, as in marshalling and directing the divisions of an army for the carrying of a fortification. No military commander attempts this by taking as they come a crowd of civilians, or of soldiers even, and leading them in such an order or disorder against a fortress. Masses of men are efficient and available only as they are skilfully separated, arranged, and brought forward. The same is true of the mental forces which are to carry any stronghold of opinion or belief, of ignorance or prejudice. Out of a medley of thoughts, reflections, facts, reasons, and imaginations, relevant and irrelevant, those available and appropriate are to be chosen, and more rejected, perhaps, than retained. How many will come from all quarters, even when the subject of discourse is clearly in mind, can with difficulty be estimated. Perhaps one in five or ten that flit through the mind is all that can be made useful for the theme in hand. When these are caught and collected there still remains the task of getting them into order, commonly called plan-making. This process has been insisted upon by every writer upon the art of public speech, from Corax to the present day. It is similar to that in any constructive art, as that of architecture or of mechanical engineering, where a structure is to be built upon the basis of well-known laws of physics, or a machine upon those of force and resistance. No builder of an edifice begins to lay foundations even until he has in mind what is the purpose of the building, whether for amusement, for trade, for education, or for worship. Much less does he attempt to put together such timber and brick and stone as may be lying about in the order that they happen to come to hand. Instead, he has before him an outline at least of the main divisions, apartments, and stories, for ever so simple and plain a house; and for the more elaborate structure he has drawings in detail and scale dimensions to the fraction of an inch. In machinery construction, minuteness of calculation is still more exact, and all the measurements are from a centre, while the problem of arranging large wheels and small, short shafts and long, for compactness and conservation of force, is akin to that which the commander has with regard to the disposition of his forces on the battle-field. Such minuteness of forethought may not always be possible or advisable to the builder of an oration, but in so far as it is to be an example of constructive art in the department of thought and its communication, it must conform to that law of prevision which is of essential utility in kindred arts and pursuits.

The value of such forethought in all cases is mainly to save ill-directed and hap-hazard toil and wasted labor, contributing as they do to ultimate failure. It is possible that the builder of a house by repeated attempts, with much nailing up and pulling down again, with much cutting too long and too short, might at last succeed in putting up a simple shelter without a plan drawn on paper. Without a general idea in his head, however, and adhered to, not much of a result would be secured with a moderate amount of material at hand. Nor will the composer of an address that is to be anything more than a rambling talk to children be likely to distinguish himself by general remarks made up of such thoughts as come in his way, thrown together in the order in which they happen to arrive. This may answer in the case of the newspaper "notes" which literary men contribute to newspapers and serials, charming in their facile discursiveness, but it will not do for the educated public speaker.   Audiences appreciate, as they demand, something of artistic value in dignified address.   They can distinguish between slipshod, careless, ill-arranged, unplanned discourse and that in which the speaker has seen the purpose and end of his speech from the beginning, and has ordered his approaches with a view to his object.   They may not discover this at first, but they will be sure to know it at last ; just as the passer-by may have little understanding of what a building is to be when he looks at the frame going up, but sees its beauty and proportion and design in the finished structure.

The desirability of a definite plan being admitted, both for the sake of the writer of a discourse and of those who shall hear it, it will be pertinent to inquire about the principles which should govern its construction.

Order is the first of these, as distinguished

from the greater or less disorder in which thoughts arise. Some order of sequence they must of necessity have, Ordering of material. as they are uttered one after another in continuous speaking; but such order may have no other characteristic than that of accidental succession. It may be the order of immigrants coming off a ship. The first to run down the plank may be a Swede, the next an Italian. After him comes a man from Ulster, followed by a Greek. A Dane treads on the heels of a Hungarian, a Frenchman pushes a Polander, and a Russian crowds a Turk. The only order is that of single file, one at a time, with an occasional overlapping. A natural order which might be established for a ship's company of such people would be the national, by which all Frenchman should herd by themselves, and Netherlanders by themselves, and so with all the rest; or again all who are bound for the West, or for the South, by themselves; or any other principle of division and aggregation might be adopted, which should group individuals upon some ground common to them. Such an order in composition may be termed that of association, as distinguished from the helter-skelter succession in which unrelated thoughts follow each other in the undisciplined mind, or in any mind when working lazily. The principle of association will be some common property or logical suggestion, made so plain to the hearer that he can trace the natural connection as easily as he would observe the reason for grouping a company of Mongolians, Caucasians, or Africans by themselves; and also for not mingling them promiscuously in making a race classification. Thoughts about tariff will not be accompanied by theological views; coinage arguments will not intrude upon literary criticism; patriotic sentiments will not suggest a study of ancient pottery; and the lessons of a noble life will not be alloyed with the political prospects of a presidential candidate.

The same is true of the thoughts upon any subject which come singly or in troops from all quarters of the universe. They must be marshalled in some order different from that of their arrival. Upon what further principle? Almost any one, it may be replied, if it is only one, and not two or three. This

Principles of arrangement.

unity is not so much a principle of order in general as the essential of any and every order in which the thoughts to be communicated can be arranged. As there can well be but one theme of a single discourse, so every branch of it must be in connection with the central idea so intimately that its unity is apparent as well as real.

It is because of this unity which prevails in the plan of every well-regulated discourse that the customary order of plan-making is in the succession of Introduction, Discussion, and Conclusion, which is *Three divi-sions of discourse.* as natural a sequence as that of morning, mid-day, and evening. Like any other undertaking it must have a beginning, a longer or shorter continuance, and an end. One of these three terms of the proportion may be dropped by the eccentric or the pretentious speaker; but something will be missed by the hearer who is not quite ready to be plunged into the thick of the argument, or who is left to make his own application of it in an abrupt ending. In spite of all new discoveries and nomenclatures, the human nature which is not new still demands the natural order of growth in discourse from a beginning to an end with increasing volume and power, and expects this as inevitably as it looks for increasing heat and denser foliage with the procession of summer days.

In the order, then, which is established by Association and Unity will follow next Growth. The opening sentiments of a discourse will be followed by stronger thoughts, and these in turn by the strongest reasons in closing. This, of course, relates only to the large and general outline, the three-fold division which belongs to the conventional and almost universal form of public address in all its history. What maxims shall have weight in the minor divisions and subdivisions of any discourse cannot be the subject of suggestion even. They belong to the realm of topic, and of personal taste, and that domain into which the orator must go without other guide than his own sense of what is fitting. He will be directed by the occasion, the cause, the character, the prospect, the retrospect. On the same occasion and in the same cause one man will proceed in one way, another in another, and both will produce similar results. · The law of liberty works in no single direction. Much plan-work, therefore, must of necessity be left to the writer's own invention. After he has determined that his main points shall be referrible to a single proposition, and that they shall succeed one another by some law of association and with increasing power, and that the thoughts which belong to the beginning shall be placed there, and those which pertain to the conclusion shall wait their turn, then the writer may use a large liberty in the disposition of his material. Better than minute directions for this or that occasion will be the study of examples of planning by wise speakers on kindred subjects and similar occasions. The careful reading and analysis of their discourses will reveal the framework on which they built masterpieces of instruction, argument, and appeal. There is no lack of such literature, and no occasion that is likely to arise is unrepresented in its marvellous variety of topic and treatment.

The time spent in elaborating the outline of discourse is by no means lost. In the first place, a marking out of the general direc- Plan prevents tion which the discussion is to take digression. is preventive of such digressions as are apt to occur when the line of argument is not clearly determined beforehand. Nothing is more uncertain than the suggestions and associations of the cogitating faculty. The ramifying tendency of rapid thinking is well known, and nothing is easier than to let one thought throw out a side branch, and this another lateral shoot, and on, and on, until the proper line and axis of growth is deserted and the discourse becomes like a tree whose branches are all turned aside and still farther away from the perpendicular which the main trunk should have followed. Indeed a large part of the discipline of composition is in the constant checking of a straying mind. Accordingly it is a great advantage to have the main line of thought so clearly laid down in advance that the thinker shall know when he is progressing directly, and also when he is off the track and far afield. If he is inclined to wander when planning his speech, it is easier to note any point of departure at a glance by reason of the compactness of his " brief " and to bring himself into line at once. It is very much as in the case of the traveller, who can lay out his journey by the map better than he can discover his best course with the whole unexplored country lying near and far, seen and unseen, before him. In the one case, he is feeling his way from point to point, sometimes taking diverging paths, sometimes losing the way altogether. In the other instance, he is careful only to make the best and most of a path which has been indicated in advance. There is no perplexity as to its directness or its termination. It is known how and where it will come out, whatever may be its undiscovered and undeveloped resources.

Proportion is a further advantage secured by a well-ordered plan. It is easy to fall into the error of disproportionate division of the main parts of a composition. *Secures proportion.* With cautious writers it is common to over-load and unduly lengthen the Introduction for fear that the material at hand, or to be gathered, will not hold out. The incautious writer is apt to commit the same mistake at the other end of his address, and draw out his Conclusion inordinately because of his improvidence or laziness in previous sections. Or, once more, the body of the discourse may be overstocked or attenuated in ideas, with little introduction, and no conclusion other than a sudden and unexpected stop. Want of time is the customary apology. The true reason is a faulty distribution of time. A ten-minute speech, in its way, can be constructed with as harmonious proportions as one of an hour in length. But whether short or long, the only security for such construction lies in the proper arrangement of the plan, and in strict adherence to its relative allotments.

An experienced writer will doubtless ask: What is to be done with those suggestions of a better way which actual composition often inspires ? The general reply is that no first draft of the outlines of a discourse is to hamper the mind in its reaching after the best plan. The preliminary sketch is rather to aid the writer in finding the best way, that is, the one which is the most direct to its object. But, the general direction being determined by the first sketch, a shorter and better road is not on this account prohibited. Many a surveyor who has submitted his preliminary route-line for a new railway, and has had it accepted, has found a shorter cut still more satisfactory when the road came to be built.   And that man who is confident that he will make no change in his house-plan while the house is building, has an uncommonly exalted opinion of his powers of prevision, higher perhaps than he has when the house is finished and he has occupied it awhile. Still, the more devising he does in advance, the better it will be for himself and the builder; and the more forethought the writer gives to his plan, the better will be the composition, and the sooner will he come to the object in view.

There must of course be taken into account the plan which the experienced writer may make as he writes, keeping the main *The skilled writer's plan.* line of his discourse always in view, and avoiding with a craftsman's intuition the danger of being diverted from his purpose. But this quick discernment and severe control constitute one of the late rewards of patient analytic and synthetic labor,—which is the best method of plan-making for a beginner. Its processes may be tedious and seemingly retarding, but in the end, when results are computed, such forethought will appear among the economies of composition.

V.

THE INTRODUCTION.

THE plan being deliberately sketched, and filled in with such minuteness as the time and accumulated material of the writer will permit, he will be impatient to construct the complete fabric of his discourse section by section. Ordinarily he will wish to begin with the opening sentences, whether he afterward keeps them unchanged or not. A provisional or experimental introduction is better than **Provisional introduction.** too much care or thought about the initial paragraph, something with which to get under way and to acquire momentum enough to give movement and life to the main body of the discourse. It may be discarded when this is secured and count no more than the preliminary " scoring " of the thoroughbred before he crosses the starting line. Still the preparatory spin has brought him to his racing pace and therefore has its value. It is much the same with the introduction which is written to give a fair "send-off."

The final and accepted introduction will, however, have certain qualities that are indispensable to so prominent a division. For it is to be observed that this portion of the discourse is probably listened to by a larger part of an audience than any subsequent section, especially if the speaker be a stranger, or if his topic be an unusual one. However much attention may be relaxed, and thoughts wander as the address lengthens, there is a general if not universal listening to the opening sentiments of the speaker. Therefore it is incumbent upon him that his words have at least a negative value, and that he does not violate, in his first paragraph, one or two common principles of good taste and of wise policy.

The first of these is the maxim of conciliation. It is a commonplace to suggest that no man can be eloquent to a disaffected audience. He may be as earnest, as logical, as skilful in argument, as elegant in diction, as strong in appeal, as under more propitious circumstances, but he will have none of these virtues in the opinion of a hostile assembly. Nor is it for the orator always to choose his auditory. The advocate at the bar cannot, and he seldom finds listeners entirely with him; sometimes they are wholly opposed to him. The same is true of the legislative assembly and the political campaign meeting. Even the minister of the Word has in his congregation dissenting elements, or he may easily create them by an unwelcome message, or an unpopular theme. It is, however, to the occasional orator, appearing perhaps as a stranger before an expectant or curious multitude, that the expediency arises of singular wisdom and close adherence to the law of conciliation, both in its positive and negative application,—not to rouse antagonism, and to allay it if already existing. To do this wisely, conciliation must not be overdone. The anxiety or willingness to propitiate is sometimes so great that the audience becomes as conscious of it as the speaker, greatly to his prejudice. There are limits, for instance, to the amount of flattering things which can safely be said to an assembly as well as to a person. It may listen, and even respond with a sort of corporate loyalty when its town, society, or state is excessively praised; but this is no indication that many do not see through an artifice which is intended to make them well disposed toward the speaker. It becomes therefore a matter of both delicacy and difficulty to secure that good understanding between orator and audience which shall preserve the self-respect of the one and win the favor of the other. This is particularly the case when the hearers, as a body or in part, are known to be opposed in sentiment, opinion, or belief to the person who is to address them. Any attempt to conciliate will be regarded with suspicion, and flattery is fatal as indicating artifice or cowardice or weakness. Defiance, though bad policy in general, is much more in keeping with the spirit of such an assembly. Savages even have a rude respect for an enemy with bravery enough to taunt them, and a howling mob will sometimes yield to the appeal for fair play, when they would not be soothed by one's praising the spark of decency that may be lurking under many layers of dirt and disagreeableness. Political and reform orators have found conciliation the first if not the greatest difficulty in winning audiences over to their cause. Succeeding or failing in this initial step, they have gained or lost their victory from the start.

It is almost superfluous to state the reason why so much importance is attached to the good nature of a company of hearers. If it were always composed of pure intellect, with judging and reasoning faculties in calm condition, capable of free and untrammelled action, there would be little need of conciliatory words, whatever the sentiments of the speaker might be. But in the natural blending of opinions and feelings, beliefs and motives, doctrines and prejudices, the emotions are the active and controlling elements, with a wonderful facility in passing themselves off as purely intellectual in character. Every observer knows how often opinion is mistaken for absolute fact, belief for truth, wilfulness for conscientiousness. Accordingly the speaker has to approach the minds of his hearers in many instances through enveloping mists of opposition, prejudice, and antipathy, to say nothing of ignorance and misinformation. To dispel such misunderstanding, remove prejudice, disarm opposition, and put the hearer on neutral ground even is no easy task; while to win him over into the orator's own province is an achievement which may well gratify one of the highest ambitions which he may cherish.

If there is a single maxim that applies to the majority of cases, it is one which advises a dignified reserve in both commendation and condemnation when there is extreme opposition, and very little of anything approaching flattery in ordinary circumstances. An audience always respects a speaker who respects himself, and they will pardon him if he does not go far out of the way to propitiate them. This does not imply, of course, that the wise man may not create a sentiment in his own favor by a skill which is so adroit that it shall seem natural and be effective. It will be found, however, that honesty and frankness appear to be, if they are not in reality, the principal features in such an appeal to the good sense of the hearers as the speaker must make in the beginning, if his subsequent discourse is to prosper with

Examples of conciliatory introductions. them. A few exemplifications of timely and gracious conciliation will illustrate the truth and value of the maxim.

When Samuel Adams addressed a large audience in Philadelphia in August, 1776, he made good terms with his hearers by saying at the outset:

" Truth loves an appeal to the common sense of mankind. Your unperverted understanding can best determine on subjects of a practical nature. Positions above the comprehension of the multitude are apt to be visionary and fruitless. He who made all men hath made the truths necessary to human happiness obvious to all."

Henry Clay in speaking for a long-established revenue system in 1832 makes common ground with his political opponent by asking, "Can we proceed to this work of destruction without a violation of public faith?" When Garfield as a Representative was about to tell the House that it had by its action resolved to enter upon a revolution against the Constitution and Government of the United States in 1879, he prefaced his speech by saying: "I wish I could be proved a false prophet in reference to the result of this action. I wish that I could be overwhelmed with the proof that I am utterly mistaken in my views." Similar concession to opposing sentiment won respectful consideration for his own reluctant and serious conviction. One of the most graceful opening sentences is that of Stephen A. Douglas's speech on the war, at Springfield, Illinois, in 1861: " I am not insensible to the patriotic motives which prompted you to do me the honor to invite me to address you upon the momentous issues now presented in the condition of the country." Two years later, when Abraham Lincoln began his Gettysburg address there was no need of conciliating the listening throng, but if there had been, his reference to the fathers who made a new nation, and to the soldiers who gave their lives that the nation might not die, would have won the multitude.

Assuming now that the audience is favorably disposed toward the speaker, either because it has no reason to be otherwise, or because he has succeeded in removing disaffection, there may yet

Indifference and its removal.

5

exist, what is of almost equal disadvantage to him, a spirit of indifference whose continuance is destructive of the best oratorial results. Indifferentism is better than opposition though worse than favor, it might be urged; but it is worse than either: for an opposing element rouses the speaker to his best effort to overcome it, but unconcern inspires nothing beyond discouragement and despair. It is a dead-weight upon the speaker's spirits. There is no rebound and no response. His words strike as bullets strike earthworks and are lost and wasted. To banish this sluggish indifference becomes, then, the next necessity for an orator. It is not needful to ask whence it comes, nor when, nor why. To a greater or less degree it may exist in every assembly; in some persons by nature, in others by present lack of interest in the theme, or by more immediate concern about something else, or by any diversion and distraction that may arise. Causes do not concern the speaker so much as preventives and remedies. How can interest be roused and attention be secured is the second problem that he is to solve.

The first step towards its solution is to establish the importance of his subject to his hearers.
Not until their personal connection
with his cause is made clear can a
profitable consideration of his words

Establishing
importance
of subject.

be depended upon. Therefore he will labor to
make the connection clear between his topic
and his audience. Its importance may be never
so great absolutely. Is it also relatively to
the company before him? If he cannot show
that it is, their attention will be only the civil-
ity of good breeding, and their patience that of
habit. The fact that a number of people have
assembled to hear what is to be said on a given
topic is a general guarantee of their interest in
it. This implies, of course, that the subject is
known beforehand, as in a lecture, or an advertised address on a public occasion. The same
is true, in a measure, of an occasion which limits
the speaker to a definite class of subjects, as the
Sunday discourse or a course of lectures, scientific or literary. The audience is somewhat
interested in anything that may be discussed
within the customary range of topics. It may
be a mild sort of interest, however, bordering

on indifference with a large portion of the assembly. If it is nothing more than mild, the
speaker may need at times to make it more.
At times, let it be observed, but not every time;
for it is easy to get into a way of making the
present subject the most important of all subjects—until the next one is announced. Preachers are particularly inclined to fall into this
habit of emphasizing unduly the present theme,
forgetting how recently they did the same, and
that a more important truth may be awaiting
them. Other public speakers also have been
known to magnify the occasion beyond its
relative value. Still there are times and topics
of unusual importance of which an audience
may not be duly sensible. To make them so,
will be a part of the speaker's business. It will
not be enough to tell them that the occasion
or the subject is momentous. They may as
well be told to be good or generous or phil-
anthropic, and with a similar result. There
must be a general or a specific reason for such
effort; and in like manner the importance of
any truth must have more than the assertion
of the speaker to impress it upon the hearer.

Therefore considerable skill is requisite to make him understand that the subject in hand is of more than ordinary consequence, or of enough at least to rouse him from the indifference which may be habitual.

This skill will take such direction as the good sense of the orator dictates. First, the occasion may help him. Webster recognized this in his famous definition of eloquence, and he himself was immensely advantaged in many instances by the associations and suggestions of the hour and the place, notably at Bunker Hill and Plymouth, as Lincoln was at Gettysburg. Such occasions are eloquent in themselves, and the orator has only to interpret their lesson and be their spokesman. They set the current of all thoughts in the same direction, while the speaker makes observations by the way. The importance of what he utters is determined as much by the occasion as by his own efforts, and these in turn are greatly helped by the tide of concordant sentiment which flows along with them. Against this drift of sympathetic feeling none but a simpleton will allow himself to oppose anything discordant, incongruous, or hostile. If he is so disposed, he should husband his resources for a more propitious time of neutrality, or of avowed opposition on the part of his hearers, and make the most of the favoring occasion and ·its present importance. Nothing indeed can be more important at the time than the occasion, not even the man who is to interpret and apply its lessons. So thought Judge Brackenridge of Philadelphia, when in 1789 he delivered a eulogy on the brave men who had fallen in the War of the Revolution: " I know my abilities rise not to a level with so great a subject, but I love the memory of the men who have risked their lives in the war of America, and it is my hope that the affection which I feel will be to me instead of genius."

If, however, the speaker be not subordinate to the occasion, and cannot be aided by it, he finds the task of impressing his auditors a more difficult one.   A man like Samuel Adams in the beginning of the speech quoted above may accomplish it in an indirect way by saying: " I would gladly have declined an honor [of speaking] to which I find myself unequal. I have not the calmness and impartiality which the infinite importance of this occasion demands." But if he had opened his address with the statement, " This is an infinitely important occasion," the effect would have been sadly marred. Chief Justice Oliver Ellsworth, in the Connecticut Convention of 1788, conveyed the right impression when he began his speech with the words: " Mr. President, this is a most important clause in the Constitution ; and the gentlemen do well to offer all the objections which they have against it." Sheridan, in his speech on the Begum Charge, approaches the topic in a novel way: " I shall not waste time by any preliminary observations on the importance of the subject before you. My friend Mr. Burke has already executed the task in a way most masterly and impressive." Lord Chatham did the same when, in his maiden speech, delivered in the House of Commons April 29, 1736, he said: " I am unable, Sir, to offer anything suitable to the dignity and importance of the subject which has not already been said by my honorable friend who made the motion." And three years later he began his speech on the Spanish Convention thus: " Sir, there certainly has never been in Parliament a matter of more high national concern than the convention referred to the consideration of this committee." And Burke had such a sense of the importance of American affairs to Great Britain that he termed the subject " an awful one, or there is none so on this side of the grave."

Examples of emphasizing the importance of the speaker's theme might be multiplied be-

Justification of the speech in introduction. yond the interest of the reader in them. Indeed, in one way or another, it is expedient, to say the least, to establish at once the claim which a topic has upon the hearer. If it does not of itself make the demand evident, then the orator's business is to make it plain before he has trespassed long upon time and attention ; and the more adroitly he does this the better will be received what he has to say further in substantiation of this claim. In fact this will become the measure of his right to speak at all. If he have no important message, he has no call to inflict himself upon an audience, unless they have come together for diversion or amusement or to be bored.

The audience being in good humor with the orator, and reasonably impressed with the importance of his subject, the introduction may end with a fuller statement of the theme and its division for discussion than it has been thus far convenient to make. In other words, the order and outline of discourse may be introduced or formally presented to the listeners. How fully and minutely is another question for the skill, tact, discretion, and wisdom of the speaker to determine. In this, too, he will be governed largely by the law of proportion, by the probable interest and expectancy of the hearer, and by a politic reserve which does not anticipate the discussion too much. Still there should be a fuller statement of the topics to be discussed than can usually be given in the title or theme-wording. These may now be expanded in the statement by enumerating the order in which the principal divisions of the discourse will be taken up, a procedure which is often helpful and gratifying to the attentive hearer. Judge Story's oration at Harvard in 1826, on "The **Examples.** Characteristics of the Age," illustrates such enumeration at the close of his introduction where he says:

"What I propose to myself on the present occasion is to trace out some of the circumstances of the age which connect themselves with the cause of science and letters ; to sketch here and there a light and shadow of our days ; to look somewhat at our own prospects and attainments, and thus lay before you something for reflection, for encouragement, and for admonition."

This is his expanded version of a theme which is simply, "The Characteristics of the Age": and in this fuller statement he outlines his entire discourse. In his memorial address on the lives of Jefferson and Adams, William Wirt, after alluding to the "consummation of their lives" in an introduction of some length, outlines his oration by saying briefly, "Let us recall the more prominent incidents of these illustrious lives," which were, as he afterward recounts them, their early studies, political tendencies, associations, and championships, congressional careers, and presidential administrations. In the speech at the trial of Aaron

Burr, 1807, the same orator makes his statement in four propositions, corresponding to the four which his opponent had made, and then adds, "I beg leave to take up these propositions in succession and give them those answers which to my mind are satisfactory." This is in accord with Quintilian's assertion that there is much attraction in an argument which derives its substance from the pleading of an opponent, for the reason that it does not appear to have been composed at home but to be produced on the spot. This of course applies more particularly to forensic efforts, although there is much in them that is applicable to public address of every kind, for in a sense each hearer is a judge before whom some sort of a cause is presented.

Such enumeration of propositions to be discussed should not, however, be too long for modern memories, nor be so minute as to leave nothing that may appear to spring spontaneously from the course of discussion. It is probable, moreover, that such ordering of the outline has its best use in indicating to the hearer the progress of the speaker as he reannounces the main propositions one after another as his speech proceeds. Like milestones, these landmarks of discourse as they are recalled and restated tell the audience how far they have come and how much farther they have to go. Sometimes an assembly is more patient than it would otherwise be when it perceives with evident relief that the last stage is not far away.

VI.

THE DISCUSSION.

THIS word, Discussion, primarily denoting debate, will be used as a general term covering the various methods of discourse employed in the body of any public address. The variety of these methods is necessarily as great as the character of different occasions, subjects, and speakers can make it.   Recognizing this almost infinite diversity, writers upon the art of oratory at an early period attempted to classify the commonest forms which were constantly recurring in social and civic life.

Aristotle, twenty-two centuries ago, with full knowledge of all that his predecessors had said and of what opinions his contemporaries held in an age of eloquence, makes a threefold division

Discussion in different kinds of discourse.

Ancient classifications of oratory.

of orations into deliberative, judicial, and demonstrative; or those which relate to the
future, the past, and the present, respectively;
things to be accomplished, or already done, or
now doing or existing; matters therefore to be
deliberated about, or judged, or condemned, or
praised.   So also he makes a threefold division
of the motive.   For deliberative oratory it is
the expedient or the inexpedient, with recommendation and dissuasion; for judicial oratory
the consideration is that of justice or injustice;
while the end of demonstrative speech is praise
or blame resulting in honor or disgrace.   Quintilian, after noticing different principles and
methods of division adopted by Anaximenes,
Protagoras, Isocrates, and other Greeks, adopts
Aristotle's division with so much change of order as to make it, first, demonstrative; second,
deliberative; third, judicial.   He also notices
the attempt of some Greek writers, whom
Pliny the elder follows in his own day, to
make it appear that there are almost innumer-
able kinds of oratory.   Against this minute
division he is driven to say that for himself he
might divide oratory into only two kinds,

judicial and extra-judicial, forensic and all others. But with his customary fairness he finally remarks that it has appeared safest to him to follow the majority of writers, and therefore he adopts the tripartite division just given. In the decline of oratory there was more or less tendency to minute division, especially in scholastic ages, until the revival of learning brought back a wholesome respect for the best methods of antiquity, although it may be said that Aristotle, Cicero, and Quintilian were always standards of authority with speakers and rhetoricians who could read the languages in which these authors wrote.

Sir Francis Bacon, in discoursing of the wisdom of the ancients, condensed something of it in his " Antitheta," or rhetorical commonplaces, acute in thought and pointed in their concise expression ; but while Modern classifications. he says nothing of the formal order of discourse he does not depart materially from the decisions of antiquity. Sir Thomas Wilson, who died forty-five years before Sir Francis Bacon, published in 1553, ten years before Shakespeare was born, his *Arte of Rhetorique*, the first text-book of composition and criticism in our language. The rules in this treatise are derived chiefly from Aristotle through Cicero and Quintilian. Two hundred years later, in 1759, Hugh Blair appeared as the next writer of eminence upon the art of discourse,—so eminent that King George the Second was induced to establish a professorship of rhetoric and polite literature at the University of Edinburgh, and to appoint Dr. Blair as its first professor. In his enumeration of the ancient division he gives a clear definition of each, following Quintilian's order. He says "the scope of the Demonstrative was to praise or to blame; that of the Deliberative to advise or to dissuade; that of the Judicial to accuse or to defend." Then he adds: " This division runs through all the ancient treatises on Rhetoric and is followed by the moderns. It is a division which comprehends most or all of the matters which can be the subject of public discourse." It suits his purpose, however, to adopt a division suggested by "the three great scenes of modern eloquence, namely, popular assemblies, the bar, and the pulpit," which he qualifies by saying that "the eloquence of the bar is precisely the same with what the ancients call the judicial; and that of the popular assembly, though mostly what they term the deliberative species, yet admits also of the demonstrative; while the eloquence of the pulpit is altogether of a distinct nature and cannot be properly reduced under any of the heads of the ancient rhetoricians." In substance, he has not forsaken the division of his Greek and Roman masters. It is a long reach from Quintilian at Rome to George Campbell at Aberdeen, and from the close of the first century of our era to the year 1766 when the *Philosophy of Rhetoric* was published. In his preface he remarks that considerable progress had been made by the Greeks and Romans in devising the proper rules of composition not only in the two sorts of poesy, epic and dramatic, but also in the three sorts of orations, the deliberative, the judicial, and the demonstrative. It will be observed here that he follows the order of Aristotle rather than that of Quintilian. He then adds: "And I must acknowledge that, as far as I have been able to discover, there

6

has been little or no improvement in this respect made by the moderns."

Eighty years later, in 1846, Richard Whately,
Archbishop of Dublin, the next prominent
Recent clas- writer upon Composition, so far as
sification. he has any division of the oration,
does not disagree with Aristotle; but he is
more concerned with address to the understanding and the will, with matters of style
and delivery, than about different kinds of
speeches. But twenty years after him, 1866,
came another Aberdeen professor with a work
which he confesses is more allied to Campbell,
Blair, and Whately than to lighter works on
English Composition. This writer was Alexander Bain, who is still held in high repute by
the latest authorities in the province of rhetoric. His classification is "according to the
different occasions of oratory"; each giving
rise to a distinct method, and constituting a
separate professional study: I. The oratory
of the law courts; II. Political oratory; III.
Pulpit oratory; IV. Moral suasion. There
can be discovered in this nomenclature a sur-
vival of Aristotle's and Quintilian's terms,—

Judicial, Deliberative, and Demonstrative, for his two last divisions are practically but one, unless moral suasion be excluded from the pulpit and confined to biography, poetry, and the novel, according to Bain's intimation. A still later division has been made by Professor Genung into I. Determinate, including forensic, parliamentary, and pulpit oratory; II. Demonstrative, or "that which impels toward noble, patriotic, and honorable sentiments and toward a large and worthy life." If, now, two of the three divisions under Determinate be called by their ancient names, we shall have for "forensic," judicial; and for "parliamentary," deliberative;—pulpit oratory not being known until the early Christian centuries. Adding Demonstrative to the other two ancient divisions, the real permanence of the great Athenian analyst's classification is apparent: Judicial, Deliberative, Demonstrative.

It is worth observing that Aristotle places Demonstrative oratory last in order, as addressed to the hearer and in the present time, while Judicial passes judgment upon what is past, and

Deliberative considers what is to come.   He also makes praise or blame the object, and honor or dishonor the result of such speech. Now if inquiry be made about the kinds of address which fall within the scope of such oratory, it will be seen that commendation and condemnation must have objects as definite as the personal deeds and character of the man, or the corporate acts of a number of men, or the events which are not beyond human control and responsibility.   Discourse of this nature will accordingly be demonstrative or epidictic in the sense of *showing forth* the true character of persons or actions, in order that such exposition may have its influence upon the hearer. In a word, it is the oratory of the object-lesson.

This being true, it is pertinent to ask about the nature of the subjects to be discussed in such oratory.   Leaving matters of litigation to judicial or forensic speech, and subjects of legislation to deliberative, and also, as a necessity, religious instruction to the pulpit, what remains for the occasional oration?   Things, it may be answered, as immaterial as the human soul, and as evanescent as the instantaneous act.

But as the thoughts of the heart issue in deeds, and deeds repeated result in character, and the character of the majority becomes that of a nation or an age, it is immensely important that the impalpable and fleeting forces which are at the foundation of the social fabric should be discerned, and that communities should be helped to discriminate between the good and the bad, between policy and principle, the honorable and the dishonorable. This they cannot always be expected to do until they are made to see the difference between good and evil. So also with motives and incentives to action. A concrete example effectively presented is worth a dozen precepts. A personal trait of character, illustrated by a striking instance of its working, inspires respect and provokes imitation and cultivation of the same more than many injunctions to obey and follow the abstract truth which it embodies or illustrates. Or, on the other hand, an evil event, an act of fraud, injustice, or iniquity, divested of its cloak and placed in strong daylight, becomes its own condemnation, and also an admonition to the public.

Besides the acts and character of prominent individuals, and the enactments of national legislatures, and the trend of public

Ethical and political subjects. opinion, and the high or low level of public morals, there is another legitimate field for the exercise of criticism by demonstrative oratory in the sphere of general truths which have a present, because an ever-lasting and constant value. What is right or honorable or beneficent or beautiful or generous or self-sacrificing or patriotic has always been recognized as such and always will be in the main features of these virtues. Belonging to a long past and having the promise of a long future, they are emphatically the possession of the present as a moving point in the procession of the years, an eternal Now. By inheritance and by the responsibility of a trust-holder for the future, the present time guards, keeps, and uses these imperishable principles of right and honor, benevolence and generosity. It is by reason of this permanence and continuity of unalterable principles that language, as the expression of common conviction, speaks of them as always in the present, as for example:

"Socrates said that the immortal *is* indestructible, and that the soul *is* immortal"—not was; the present tense, not the past.

There is, then, no lack of subject-matter in demonstrative oratory. Literally its field is as wide as the world of universal truth and as specific as personal character. If a speaker can afford to do it, and is able to do it profitably, he may roam at large over a boundless range of universal and timeless truth, or again, if he choose and can do it, he may describe a small circle in this wide field and sink a shaft like a well into the depths of a single character, or of a single act, opinion, sentiment of any community, nation, or age. Extensively, therefore, or intensively he may work according to his will and courage, his choice and ability, or according to the need of the audience and the suggestion of the occasion. But he will take care to bring out of the length and breadth of the wide domain of perpetual truth, or out of its heights and depths, things which may be set before his hearers for ideals to follow or for examples to shun.

The demonstrative treatment of such themes

has methods as peculiarly its own as those of the
court-room, the legislative hall, or the
pulpit.   If the word demonstrative
or, as the Greeks had it, epidictic, has
a primary meaning not conveyed in our present
use of the term, it is the idea and the act of pointing out and exhibiting,—a sense which is sometimes lost in that of demonstration by argument
and proof, so called. To exhibit, therefore, what
is, or to point out what needs only to be seen in
order to be admitted, is the import of the term.
Such exhibition and revelation requires methods distinct, definite, and appropriate to the undertaking. For there are hundreds of truths
clothed in concrete form and existing on every
hand which are powerless, or less powerful than
they might be, because they are unrecognized
and uninterpreted. They pass in and out among
men in commonplace disguise.

A primary qualification, therefore, of the
demonstrative orator is that he be somewhat
of a discoverer. He must find what
is not commonly seen, or unveil
what is but dimly discerned by the heedless.
The ability to do this may be the gift of a seer

Its methods are expository.

The orator a discoverer.

only, but, possessed in any degree, it may be cultivated. The sublime vision from the field of Zophim was seen by the diviner of Midian whose eyes had been shut but now were open. So the open vision may come sometimes by diligent cultivation to one who at first saw imperfectly. In some degree, then, the orator must have the perceptive faculty developed, and his success will largely depend upon its exercise. To see the unseen and to find what is hidden from the unobservant is the foundation of demonstrative discourse; for how can the speaker point out what he himself has not found, and what every one sees beforehand needs no exposition. Such discernment is greatly sharpened by the habit of observation. By this is not meant a casual notice of occurrences and facts, but rather the prolonged study which attends inductive processes, where similarities in things dissimilar are discovered, and causes are traced from effects and results are seen to follow precedent action. It is a searching and investigating process which, patiently pursued, will result in discovery in the fields pertaining to demonstrative speech as surely as in the domain of any other science. Such perception may be intuitive in a great dramatist or a great orator, but in most men it is the result of cultivating the observant and perceptive faculties which are seldom entirely lacking in any person.

In its operation it is known among rhetoricians as Invention, a word which to modern **Invention.**   understandings has a sense partly of creation and partly of discovery, and is best apprehended when applied to a new combination of matter, as in a machine, and is most frequently associated with the modern meaning of patent, as in a patented invention.   In Cicero's day, however, and how much earlier it is not easy to say, he who "invented" "came upon" an idea, a thought, a perception, a quality, a trait of character in man or race, the meaning of an event, a drift of sentiment, a tendency of an age.   He might "meet with" it by chance or more likely "find" it after much searching ; but when found it was his Invention, and the finding process was called by the same name, which altered conditions have so changed in meaning as to warrant and perhaps demand this notice of the change in the word itself. Meantime the Latin signification has lived on with the treatises in which the word is embalmed.

It has been the custom of some writers in recent years to assert that Invention is beyond the limits of rhetoric proper, which, they add, is concerned with modes of expression only. The best writers of antiquity did not think so. Their large views of the art of rhetoric may indeed be safely narrowed so as not to include the entire circle of human knowledge as they then did; but in doing this care is to be taken not to eliminate one of the two essential factors in the process of composition. For there must be a thought to communicate antecedent to any method of communication, as a person generally thinks before he speaks. This thought may be called an accumulation from which to select the material of discourse, and not the discourse itself, or it may be ruled out as antecedent and preliminary to the act of composition; but he will be a most remarkable writer who can go far along in his discourse without hav-

ing to renew his inventive process, however
complete his preparation may have been. To
separate invention from composition is like
separating the gathering of stone, brick, iron,
and wood from the building process. Provide
beforehand as he may, every builder knows
that much more will have to be collected as the
edifice goes up, and he does not discriminate
between the labor and cost of finding material
and incorporating it into the structure. So let
any one who is composing say, if he can, that
the moments he has spent in finding a thought
were no part of the time taken to express that
thought, and therefore not to be reckoned as
composition, which upon this theory relates entirely to words and their arrangement. Instead
of this, it is safe to say that invention, or
thought-gathering, is the primary if not the
principal part of composition, and if done well
makes later processes easy and effective. If it is
ill done, no choice of words, no elegance of diction, no graces of figurative language can make
good the loss, as no elaboration of external
ornament can atone for the absence of solid
foundations and strong walls in a building.

And as thought and words are inseparably joined together in the mind, and in conversation so intimately connected as to go hand in hand, so in writing and in public speaking, especially in extemporaneous speaking, they cannot be divorced except by a refinement of abstraction which is worthy of an eleventh-century schoolman. Sir Francis Bacon in the beginning of the seventeenth century did indeed assert in his *Advancement of Learning* that "to invent is to discover that we know not, and the use of this invention is no other but out of the knowledge whereof our mind is already possessed, to draw forth or call before us that which may be pertinent to the purpose which we take into consideration," as a remembrance or suggestion. But practically in almost all high discourse there are many things which were not known or thought when the composition of it was begun, or when the speech was begun, if in any degree extemporaneous. And if there is a stock fund of knowledge that can thus be drawn upon it must have been discovered, invented, or met with as a foundation for subsequent use.

Observation, perception, and invention are,

then, one and all, the essential preliminaries to
demonstrative oratory ; and the ora-
tor must be a discoverer before he
can find something to exhibit that is
worthy of an expenditure of attention and time
by the listener.   What can you offer us that we
have not seen and do not know already? is the
question which every audience has a right to
ask of any man who stands before it with the
implied offer of something worth the hour surrendered, multiplied by the number of his
hearers.   What new truth have you discovered? or to make a more reasonable request,
What new combination or restatement of old
truths, or what larger revelation of a hitherto
half-perceived truth, can you present?   Or can
you bring out into strong relief a fact, trait, or
tendency that we have been dimly conscious
of, but have passed by unheeded?   Such interrogations the speaker should first put to himself; for if the audience does not get a satisfactory answer in one way or another, it will
have its own revenge in the future and be conspicuous by its absence when this particular
speaker proffers his next invention.

New combi-
nations de-
manded.

The subjects of demonstrative oratory being of the character intimated above, and the necessity of keen observation and diligent invention being admitted, it will be in order to ask, What are the

modes of composition which best suit the presentation of the orator's findings? The word which defines this kind of discourse will suggest an answer. As the speech is demonstrative, the method of the discussion must be that which best shows forth its matter. Therefore, it will be expository in character, setting out for inspection the truths that have been discovered, and literally exposing them to public gaze. This will be the general method. But this exposition will include processes which precede or follow the technical exposition of the rhetoricians according to the nature and requirements of the subject under consideration. In some themes of occasional discourse the orator will need, above all, to exercise the faculty of re-presentation to others. By this is meant the ability to make others see as he sees, and to understand as he understands. In a material way it is the work of the painter who puts upon canvas the picture that is in his mind, the appearance which a landscape or human face has to his vision. He re-presents it to all beholders. The orator does the same, with words for media instead of colors. As media, words have the advantage of colors in presenting the subjects with which a speaker has oftenest to deal. At least such verbal presentation will be found inseparable from themes as objective as personal character. Let the Memorial Address or Commemorative Discourse be taken as an illustrative type of the value of descriptive writing. That which is to be re-presented is as intangible and yet as real as personal traits, the like of which every hearer has observed in various degree and combination. But the speaker's business on some particular occasion is to show what traits were predominant in a certain character, and in what degree, and with what result. If he could paint the rainbow he could not depict such a character in colors. He may do it in words.

For instance, when George Bancroft pronounced a eulogy on Andrew Jackson, a man whom he admired, he portrayed immaterial qualities with the fidelity of an artist. Sincerity, personal and moral courage, intuitive possession of creative ideas expressed with intrepidity and enforced with dauntless will, nerves of steel, and a steadfast mind were the invisible traits which were known by their outcome in action to all men, but were themselves depicted by the seer who beheld motives and characteristics apart from their outward expression. When George S. Hilliard took up the character of another military man, General Taylor, there was a similar representation of those qualities which made him great to his eulogist ; " genius and courage in battle, humane ministration when it was over, self-reliance, consciousness of strength, a stony will, an iron purpose, a reanimating spirit, 'the rock of the battle-field,'"—all these are sketched with a boldness that makes the reader see the man plainer than on canvas : for there the sturdy face and the regulation uniform only are visible, and these in the one mood of repose. No one knows better than the genuine artist the limitations of pencil and brush. His battle-fields are the scenes of one particular instant in the long day's fighting, and of necessity are the work of memory and imagination, reproducing a snap-shot of impression.   What could a clicking camera on the field of battle have accomplished in comparison with Victor Hugo's word-picturing of the great conflict of the nations at Waterloo, or with Carlyle's description of Torgau, Liegnitz, or Hohenfriedberg, in the second Silesian War?

Portraiture is not more satisfactory.   Painting is an art which may disclose something of temper and character, but what portrait can compete with a well-written biography in giving the sum and substance of a life?   Read, for example, those four sketches which Charles Sumner made of his four friends, Pickering, Story, Allston, and Channing, and then study their portraits to see which will give the better conception of character.   Or what more suggestive studies of the statesmen of his time can be found than the memorial addresses which the late Senator Anthony made in Congress as one after another of his peers dropped away? No face is so familiar to all Americans as that of Washington, but it remained for Edward

Everett to set forth traits which all the canvases together do not reveal. The same may be said of Lincoln when some master hand and pen shall gather into one harmonious and proportionate estimate the hundreds of sketches which have been made from as many points of view.

It may be conceded, then, that the occasional orator has the best medium at his command for the representation and reproduction of the immaterial and elusive *Words as media.* elements with which it is his privilege to deal on public occasions. The province is shared only by the biographer, and by him in a different way and very often with a different result. For it is the eulogist's business to portray the daily deeds and abiding principles in such a manner as to inspire all who listen with a desire to imitate the noble example which has been set before them. The precept is as old as Isocrates's time : " If you emulate a man's fame, copy his actions." The impulse may be slight and the impression trifling, but such exposition of the best in human nature and of its possibilities may be one of the shaping forces of

character for some impressible listener. The
jar is slight and the angle of deflection is small
when a train is turned aside from the line on
which it has been running, but the ultimate
divergence may be as wide apart as from the
Atlantic to the Pacific. It is not improbable
that some person who heard Blaine's eulogy on
Garfield was diverted from selfish political ambition to the higher aspiration for a broader
and better service of country and humanity.
Certainly none could have heard Curtis's eulogy
on Wendell Phillips without a thought of the
grandeur of consecration to a cause which was
none the less worthy because unpopular, and
surely not without the impulse to enter upon a
crusade against evils which are waiting for some
preacher from Picardy or Clairvaux.

VII.

THE CONCLUSION OF AN ADDRESS.

IN some particulars the Peroration is the most important division of the discourse. Other portions have their special function—to state, convince, persuade; this one has something of the office of every other. Each section has been work-
Importance of the peroration.
ing in its own way toward effecting a certain result; this one is to combine the several efforts in a final and forcible and brief presentation of the whole subject. Therefore, the speaker will have strongly in mind his purpose in speaking. He is approaching the moment when the result he has been aiming at is to be accomplished. Towards this, all that has gone before has been contributing—the truth to be established, the proposition to be proved, the moral to be in-culcated, the memory to be renewed and per-

petuated, the new purpose to be instilled, the higher level of living to be commended. In judicial oratory it would be the verdict to be secured; in deliberative, the vote to be cast or the measure to be adopted.

As a consequence of a clear view of his object, in these final paragraphs the orator will also have his subject in mind, all the more definitely for the full treatment it has just received. He cannot here be oblivious to the general course of the discussion—its narration, exposition, and argument, nor be unmindful of motives which have been addressed for persuasion to action. Thus the conclusion becomes an epitome and summary of the entire discourse. Accordingly its character will be chiefly retrospective, as what has preceded it has been prospective. But all prospectiveness should be ended by the time the peroration is reached. If fresher or better thoughts arrive late they will be rigorously excluded or crowded back into the body of the discourse, possibly to the crowding out of less valuable material. For if admitted into the peroration their very excellence may obliterate the memory of much that has taken time to speak and pains to hear. Being thus retrospective, the peroration will gather into a brief space the weight of all that has been said. This does not imply repetition, reiteration, and consequent prolixity. It is rather an assembling of comprehensive sentences which shall stand for entire sections, like centres of gravity representing at a single point the bulk of bodies.

The formal method of doing this is by recapitulation, enumerating heads and topics, a swift survey of the ground gone over. Too much formality, how- *Recapitulation.* ever, will be out of place here. The time has passed for statement of plan. Parallel lines of exposition and argument, of illustration and persuasion, have been previously laid ; they are now to converge at one point through which, as through strands twisted together, are to pass united currents of instruction, conviction, and persuasion for final impact and impulse with the concentrated force of a hundred paragraphs. Therefore the speaker's words will be suggestive rather than reiterative. It is the place for artistic dealing with the spirit of his discourse rather than with the letter of it. It is the time for employing his best skill and his whole strength in fusing together conclusions and impressions, and welding into a single bolt all the facts, reasons, and motives which he has been marshalling in their proper order.

This massing of forces for a final impression is in accordance with a law of wide application, by which the last stage of whatever has a cumulative movement is its most efficient stage. Continuous utterance of growing thought with stronger reasons, increasing interest, and augmented feeling, acquires a momentum analogous to that produced by gravitation. Its final velocity and impact should be equal to the sum of all the forces that have preceded it, accelerated by the sympathy which works toward a climax in any receptive and responsive audience that is fairly treated by a speaker. It is also in accord with another law of the human intellect which requires that the discussion of any subject shall increase in interest as it is prolonged. Otherwise there will be nothing to counterbalance the inevitable weariness, restlessness, and drowsiness which the act of listening induces. The spirit of eloquence is pitted against the spirit of slumber, with the odds in favor of the latter. Doubly fatal is the error of reversing the law of cumulation by being more interesting at the start than afterward, adding to growing weariness of the hearer an increasing tiresomeness of the speaker, ending in listless, uneasy impatience. For every reason, then, the orator will see to it that the interest in his subject and object is deepest at the close of his discourse. The chief contributor to this will be the condensed force of the entire address culminating in an impression as complete and comprehensive as the limitations of language will permit.

A final excellence in the conclusion is the evidence that the speaker knows when to stop. The conclusion is a place of peril. Few things are more exasperating to hearers than to have their expectation of the end of a discourse deferred when the hearer has led them to believe or hope that it is near. The temptation is always great to say one thing more, to add a "lastly," a "finally," and an "in conclusion," with the "single remark in closing." • It is a wise man who knows exactly when it is flood-tide in his speech and can stop before the ebb begins. Of one thing he may be sure, that if at this point his object has not been accomplished he will gain nothing by multiplying words.

In general, then, the peroration will be relatively brief and comprehensively suggestive of the entire speech. It may be needful to crowd it with strong and stirring words appealing to lofty motives. And whatever may have been the taste of the ancients, the modern audience will expect the speaker to stop when he reaches his highest level, rather than to keep on until he has said his last possible word and tired out his last listener.

PART II.

QUALITIES OF EXPRESSION.

I.

CARDINAL PROCESSES.

THE fundamental laws which underlie all composition manifest themselves in various forms in different kinds of literature, as the principles of life and growth in nature reveal their activity in divers ways. In like manner the creative faculty has one method of procedure in historical writing, another in scientific, and still another in imaginative, or in poetic writing. Public address also has its own processes of composition, which it shares with some, and does not share with other **Descriptive, narrative, and expository treatment.** departments of literature. With these cardinal processes should go those qualities of style which contribute largely to the effectiveness of oral discourse. Differing widely as occasional addresses do in their author, occasion, purpose, and subject, there may nevertheless be found a predominance of descriptive, narrative, and expository treatment in most of them. Facts are made to tell their own story, and traits of character are woven into the fabric of eulogy. There may be argument at times, but oftener it is a moving scene on which succeeding events of a life or an age are portrayed, growing in interest and power with the years and the decades. The narrative is not mere recounting and the description mere enumeration. Particulars which by themselves are as bare of interest as those of an abridged biographical dictionary may underlie the eulogy, and annals as dreary as those of the Anglo-Saxon Chronicle may form the substratum of a commemorative discourse ; but the compositions themselves may be splendid as Everett's eulogy upon Washington, or Curtis's upon Phillips, or Webster's orations at Bunker Hill and Plymouth, or Lincoln's epitaphian discourse at Gettysburg, and worthy of Pericles's funeral oration over the citizens slain in the first year of the Peloponnesian War.

With the narrative and expository methods there may also be combined such forms of reasoning as may be needed for the conviction which must precede persuasion; but the farther they are removed from all appearance of logical formality the more effective will they be. There is Appropriate argumentative forms. always some prejudice against the syllogism and those scholastic subtleties whose value depends entirely upon the truth of a premise or the honesty of a conclusion. In case, however, that reasoning processes must be used, they should be of the briefer and plainer sort, easily apprehended by people whose sustained attention to anything cannot be counted upon : testimony in its stronger forms, cause and effect, the *a fortiori* so frequently used in the Bible, analogies for what they are worth as illuminators, reduction to a single alternative and to the absurd, and, most pleasing of all to an audience, the destructive dilemma, between whose two horns there is as little choice as remains for the prostrate and disarmed matadore in a bull-fight. Any of these are worth more in our day than chains of reasoning which, long drawn out, are by no means "linked sweetness" to the ordinary hearer. To the followers of Chrysippus there is a peculiar delight in the Epicheirema and the Sorites' progressive or regressive, but the average listener cares little whether the syllogistic mood be Cesare, Camestres, Festino, or Baroco. Probably he would have as much sympathy with the negative figure Bocardo as any: "Some syllogisms are not regular; But all syllogisms are things important; Therefore, some things important are not regular." Or he might prefer Ferison: "No truth is without result; Some truths are misunderstood; Therefore, some things misunderstood are not without results,"—a conclusion which is often true in logical processes applied to an audience, the result being to mystify, rather than convince, and to tire rather than persuade.

More agreeable to an assembly and more effective, as well as more creditable to the speaker, is the citation of examples, *Examples and historical parallels.* or the drawing of historical parallels, a method of conviction that has been employed with great success by the best orators. The appeal to similar cases in the past has all the weight of a historical precedent. It is a fact, and not a thought-process. The record of it is in the books, often in the memory of the hearer, or if not it has somewhat of the interest of a fresh story, and moreover adds something of weight and authority to the man who has the event in his mind, and who has, furthermore, the faculty of associating events far removed from each other in time and place. It is an extension of the comparative power which finds similes and metaphors to illumine and enforce, and at the same time avoids the charge of unimaginative minds concerning imaginative discourse by dealing with historic events and persons. Speaking of our Civil War, Phillips said in 1861 : " It finds no parallel nearer than that of the Catholic and Huguenot in France, or that of the Aristocrat and Republican in 1790, or of Cromwell and the Irish when victory meant extermination. While it lasts it will have the same effect on the nation as that war between blind loyalty represented by the Stuart family, and the free spirit of the English Constitution, which kept England a second-rate power almost a century."

The difficulty in this method is for the

speaker to find parallels sufficiently exact, and the danger to the hearer is in not being able *Limitations in their use.* to determine at once whether or not the conditions of similarity are numerous enough to constitute an historical identity in the principles involved. But in honest hands and with an intelligent audience this means of conviction is both effective and interesting. How interesting and how effective let the tradition of the scene in the Virginia House of Burgesses testify, when Patrick Henry exclaimed, "Cæsar had his Brutus, Charles I. his Cromwell." The cry of "Treason, Treason" arose on all sides before he could add, " and let George the Third profit by their example."

In giving preference to the simpler and more obvious methods of proof and refutation, no *The simpler logical forms.* slight is intended to the value and utility of some logical processes, when they may be needed, as in judicial and deliberative discussion. The plea is instead for the easily understood and readily apprehended forms of conviction in demonstrative oratory, where the audience expects to be convinced or, oftener, to have its convictions fortified and confirmed rather than radically changed by the speaker. If, however, this last course becomes necessary and possible the orator should look over his logical armory with care to see if what he learned in the schools has become rusty with disuse. Above all he will see to it that he is not betrayed into the sophistries which have always done much to divorce reasoning from rhetoric, and to bring discredit upon both the art of thinking and of speaking. Always, too, it is to be borne in mind that positive proof belongs chiefly to mathematical science, and probable proof to everything else, and that every hearer has the personal prerogative of reasonable doubt. Accordingly, that form of convincing will often appeal to him most effectually which has the least appearance of art and of strenuous endeavor to convince ; a process of which it may be said once more that it is out of harmony with occasional discourse, however useful and essential it may be in the courts, in the legislative assembly, and, very rarely, in the pulpit. But the reasonableness that appeals to common sense, and abides with the second thought and sober judgment, which are sure to assert themselves eventually, is always in order.

It would be possible to say much more with reference to conviction, but its methods must always be largely a matter of individual taste and choice, in which, as in all things relating to discourse, the skill of the speaker will show itself according to his ability. The test of excellence will be in its efficiency, and that method of conviction will be best which best convinces the particular audience addressed.

Conviction in order to persuasion. Conviction there must be before persuasion; that is, if persuasion is a part of the orator's purpose here, as it always is in judicial and deliberative oratory. As all public speech has a purpose to accomplish, it may be taken for granted that as in the eulogy and commemorative address there is some purpose, so in even the more general discourse there is enough of an end to be secured to demand something of the art of persuasion and its correlative dissuasion. Indeed, this is in many cases the object of all other forms of composition in the entire discourse, as the old rhetoricians asserted. The term "persuasion" enters into the definitions of Plato, Socrates, Aristotle, Cicero, and Quintilian, and their followers in every age agree with these masters. Bacon and Campbell, Blair and Whately insist upon this persuasive element as essential to public speech. Its object is to direct the opinion and Motives, low and high. action of people by addressing motives which move the popular will. To vote for a certain man or measure, to support a given policy, to contribute to a specified charity, are examples of objects to which collective or personal action may be directed by persuasion. To be successful it must be shown that such a vote, support, or beneficence is practicable, expedient, desirable, or advantageous. These, to be sure, are inferior motives, but they are the strongest considerations with many persons, and are not without weight with all. At least they may be employed as stepping-stones to the higher motives. That which is reasonable or prudential is strong in commendation of itself to all who pride themselves upon being wise and prudent. However irrational and unwise men may be they like to be considered as the embodiment, of fairness and sagacity, and as not much influenced by their emotions. Accordingly, an appeal can be more openly made to their understanding, reason, and judgment than to their sensibilities. None the less, however, may these last motives be addressed if the appeal be adroitly made. They are mighty movers, these emotions. The love of friends and home and country; the hate of the enemies of these sacred things; the fear of calamity and disaster to body, to reputation, and to prosperity, —these are some of the strongest motives to which the speaker may direct the current of his thought. The orator who answers to Cato's definition of " a good man skilled in speaking " will of course keep to the high and noble sensibilities, avoiding the lower. However degraded a hearer may be he does not feel complimented when his revenge, envy, jealousy, avarice, and hatred of good are appealed to. Even thieves and brigands prefer to have their proverbial moiety of honor and their scanty chivalry addressed.

In this appeal to what is best there will be

a leading up to ethical motives of the highest order which are seldom quite absent from any person, and are abundant and strong with the major part of any audience. The collective conscience is often stronger than its individual elements when dis- persed and scattered. It is like the sympathetic motion of an assembly, created by contiguity and multiplied by propinquity, flaming as a hundred fagots flame when piled together, which apart, by themselves, flicker, smoulder, and go out. It is in the assembled throng, too, that the conscience of the better element stands for that of all, and the speaker can afford to address the highest motives of the best present. Humanity, philanthrophy, the welfare of others, the service of mankind, reverence of the Creator, gratitude for blessings, and a sense of corresponding obligation, culminating in devotion and service,—all these are considerations which may be presented to most persons without fear of repudiation, or of apprehension that they will have little effect at the time in moving the wills of many. Other motives may supplant these subsequently, for this the orator cannot be held responsible. Only for his hour, and his contribution to the aggregate sum of influences, is he answerable, according to his opportunity and his ability.

Persuasion, then, is in a word the management of moving principles—the powers which result in action. To make a man choose one course and abandon another, to adhere to this company and forsake that one, to vote for this measure and against the other, to adopt this policy and abjure the opposite, to cultivate integrity, truth, sobriety, benevolence, good-will, reverence, loyalty, gratitude, devotion, and to turn away from their contraries,—all this and more is the legitimate object of persuasion, and the highest achievement of the man who speaks to his fellows.

Persuasion ending in action.

II.

PERSPICUITY.

IN the foregoing chapters the Oration has been considered in its main divisions of Introduction, Statement, Discussion, and Conclusion, and by reference to its literature the chief principles which should govern its composition have been illustrated. Meantime, whatever pertains to the style of oratorical expression has been purposely deferred, for the reason that frame-work construction is better considered by itself and apart from what may be termed, in relation to it, the outer finish. Moreover, it will be observed that what has been said thus far relates chiefly to the ordering of thoughts in effective array, and belongs to the earlier stages of the orator's work. There is, however, a later process of almost equal importance—some will

Arrangement of thought and its expression.

say of even greater importance under certain conditions. However this may be, of the two elements of public address—thought and its ultimate expression—the last deserves its own share of attention.

It must be premised at the start that an exhaustive treatment of the qualities belonging to oratorical composition would be superfluous for those who have advanced so far in English composition as to undertake the writing of an extended oration. By that time they have become familiar, through text-books and instructors, with elementary rules and precepts which apply to a correct and clear construction of sentences, paragraphs, and short compositions of various kinds. These fundamental maxims will not of course be disregarded in the higher class of writing. The offence there would be greater. Grammatical errors for instance, like mistakes in spelling, are a blemish, in an essay or story, intended only for the reviser's eye, but when spoken to an audience the mistake is published to hundreds. It is a severe but true judgment which some one has pronounced, that while correct speech is no virtue, incorrect speech is a crime.

In public address pronunciation also should be included in the above sentence. This is too important a matter to be passed over without emphasizing the demand that a speaker shall conform to the best standards. By reason of diversity and disagreement among authorities, not the best, many find an apology for usages that are more varied than defensible. In the schools there is apt to be less attention paid to this branch of expression than to those which appear in writing and in print, to be seen by the instructor or the reader. When however, the graduate of school or college meets his almost inevitable fate—to speak in public,—he will betray the antecedents of his education in orthoepy within five minutes, possibly five sentences. Correct pronunciation, to be sure, is the attainment of years and the concern of a lifetime, because good usage is not immutable ; but there are those who know what it is in any year. Lexicography as a progressive science is of great value to the student of spoken language when the orthoepic department of its vocabularies is trustworthy. Still, there is a choice in dictionaries. Beyond these there is also a shade of expression at times which no key-words can indicate. On the other hand, absolute correctness is not an excellence which Americans need to import from abroad. It is a virtue which can be cultivated at home, as it has been by our best speakers with creditable results. Above all, foreign provincialisms and local accents ought not to be mistaken for standard English, written and spoken. No additions are needed to indigenous growths.

Taking it for granted, then, that the orator has passed through the primary stages of orthoepy, syntax, and the elemental principles of good usage, the immediately following pages will discuss some of the features which belong particularly to the expression in public of thought which has been previously ordered, arranged, and written out wholly or in part. In doing this it must not be understood that what is recommended may not be of value in other departments of composition as well. For example, the first quality to be commended is so important in every kind of writing that to omit its consideration here would be a glaring defect. Clearness or perspicuity ought not to need commendation to any who wish to communicate their thoughts to others; but there are several reasons for believing that this quality of style cannot be too often recommended.

Perspicuity as a primary quality of oratorical style has its necessity in the essential conditions of public speech. On the one side there is commonly a continuous and progressive utterance; on the other a listening with more or less attention, and with no opportunity of requesting a restatement of what has escaped notice or baffled understanding. In so far as a speaker does not command constant attention, or does not make himself clearly understood at once, he fails in that degree of the purpose for which he is speaking.

Necessity of clearness.

With the reader, as contrasted with the hearer, there is always the opportunity of turning back upon an obscurity in diction; but the listener must catch the speaker's meaning immediately, or lose it beyond recall. Therefore, Quintilian's precept will bear quoting once more, to the effect that the audience should not merely be able to understand what is said, but not be able to misunderstand it. This degree of perspicuity comes only as the result of much painstaking, so varied is the capacity of hearers, and so many are the distractions to which they are subject. Absolute perfection in this quality is as impossible as in others; but the advantage of approaching complete clearness is greater than similar attainment in some other and less essential features of style.

It should be remarked here that absolute clearness is one thing to a cultivated auditory and another to an uncultivated one. *Perspicuity and precision.* Or again the technical diction which is perspicuous to a professional audience is far from intelligible to laymen, as will be evident by a perusal of the following example:

"He speaks of hyperschene as abundant and gives extinction angles for the plagioclase from which he concludes that they must be very basic,—' from labradorite to anorthite.' According to him orthoclase only occurs as the large tabular phenocrysts, which is certainly not the case with my specimens."

Any geologist can render this into intelligible English, but not in as few lines without specimens at hand. In the next example it may be doubted if clearness would have been profitable to the patient, while the precision of this statement must have been fatal if heard by the victim :

" This man is an octogenarian suffering from spondylarthritis, mitral regurgitation, œdema and extreme anasarca, who had the following semeiography and applied to the hospital for paracentesis. On August 4th he suffered from borborygmus, which he attributed to lactic fermentation in the jejunum. On August 8th, however, œdema set in with dyspnœa suggesting the possibility of a complication in tricuspid insufficiency, or a large serous effusion into the peritoneal cavity for which his only chance of relief lies in the operation of paracentesis, which will now be performed."

Clearness of expression is dependent mainly upon clearness of thought. A misty conception can never be made perspicuous even by simple words. The vagueness may be made apparent by them, *Clear thought helps clear expression.* or possibly be reduced somewhat; but if the thought is not definite and distinct the expression will not be. Words will not convey more than they are charged with. They often have a suggestive power, but their representative ability at best can never be quite equal to the sight of the eyes and the vision of the mind.

Accordingly, these should be clear and strong. And the chief labor for perspicuity will be in the direction of distinct, exact, and definite views of objects and subjects. When these views are obtained the difficulty of unambiguous expression is greatly reduced for those who can command a vocabulary of reasonable fulness.

If it be asked how this primary clearness of thought is to be obtained, there is but one general answer that is applicable to all sorts of thinkers; for there are those who come to a certain conclusion by intuition and quick perception, and others again by slow procession of observation and reasoning. Patient, concentrated, and interested application of the mind is the only process by which its first clouded vision of things can be clarified. This proceeding has its analogy in the sight of the eyes. As soon as one goes beyond things familiar, or into dusk and darkness with familiar objects around him, he must gaze long and steadily before he "makes out" their substance and form. It is said that a well-trained burglar has remarkable powers of this kind in a dark room. The secret of his skill is in his patient attention to obscurities, and in waiting for such light as may be latent around him, in the absence of any other. By a similar intentness a vague thought will gradually assume definiteness, and the truth which was incomplete and indistinct will reveal itself clearly to the patient watcher. In this time of waiting something may be gained by preliminary and experimental use of the pen, especially by those who do not easily hold a continuous thought-process in mind, or prefer to secure each point in black and white as it moves on. Any device or expedient is commendable which contributes to final perspicuity. Among the most serviceable is the statement to one's self in the plainest colloquial terms the writer's apprehension of the truth, so far as it has discovered itself to him ; or better still, conversation with a friend about it, with the additional advantage of obtaining another's views. Daylight and a walk in the open air, amid the forms of nature or the business of a practical world, are often corrective of conclusions which have been formed by lamplight and in the seclusion of a study. Books

9

containing permanent values in the clarified thoughts of recognized authorities are not to be overlooked in the search for clear and definite conceptions. But with all these aids to reflection the distinctness of the final product will depend upon prolonged fixedness of the mind with steadfast gaze upon the growing object before it. In proportion as it becomes clear to the beholder will he find words to make his thought clear to others.

Still there is a choice in words, and in the felicity of choice lies the second element of **Perspicuous diction.** perspicuity. This, too, is a relative matter according to the intelligence of the hearer. It is well to " speak the thoughts of the wise in the language of the simple " if it will convey such thoughts fully and accurately to those who delight in wisdom. Unfortunately our mother-tongue in its simplest forms does not adequately represent high thinking. The Northern element in it is good for hearth and home thoughts, for sea-going and sword-wielding, for enterprise and for empire-making —in a word, for action. But the surroundings of the Saxon did not favor conquests in the realm of thought, as did those of the Hellenic and Italic races, making these languages vehicles of that reflection which succeeds primitive activity. When people pass from the one mood to the other they will repeat the experience of civilization, and require the derived rather than the home-made word to express their grown-up thought. John Bunyan did all that could be done with household words in the domain of Scriptural truth in its application to the personal life. John Milton showed that when these same truths are to be treated on loftier planes all the legacies are needed which the Anglo-Saxon has received from the Mediterranean shores and from the Orient.

In the diversity of attainment which is found in the ordinary audience the safer example is doubtless Bunyan's, especially when Milton's prose is considered, which he himself regarded as his "left-hand writing." So the impersonal auditor, who must represent the intellectual centre of the audience, will be the speaker's ideal of the average man. Him he will address in words which will convey with lucidity the thought to be communicated. His knowledge, judgment, and good taste will be in demand in every case; also the good sense always to shun a foreign word as he would a foreign manner and imported accent; to keep at a distance an intrusive provincialism as he would the dialect of the mountains or the plains; also to let the obsolete word rest after its usefulness is past and its life over, and to decline to introduce a new word as he would to present a stranger from parts unknown or to pass a coin on which no mint had placed its stamp. The one authority in diction for the speaker, more than for all other literary workmen, will be the usage of the best of his craft.

Accordingly, he is open at one more point to criticism by his hearers, who are continually *Popular criticism.* qualifying themselves to be critics of pronunciation, for instance, by hearing other speakers, by consulting authorities, and by discoveries which word-hunters are frequently publishing in newspapers for everybody to read, and to apply to the public speaker with the daring of the fish-woman toward the Attic orator who misplaced an accent. The diffusion of all kinds of information has made widespread knowledge almost as dangerous a thing as the proverbial little; for dispersed acuteness is always skipping here and there to prod superior learning at an unguarded point.

In the traditional warfare between perspicuity and precision the orator will have another opportunity to strike a balance between the exactness which requires a technical, obscure, or condensed term, and the less precise but more intelligible phrase even though prolix. At one time or another he will find that he can make no statement in ordinary words to which some one may not take exception. Young writers are most sensitive to such possible captiousness, and frequently attempt to fortify every statement at all points. Hence the temptation to employ incontrovertible terms with the risk of incomprehensibility. Better is it to take the other risk of being questioned than to be unintelligible. For with every precaution of exactness in the speaker's language, the carping critic will find the joints in the harness of mail, or the vulnerable heel of Achilles. Therefore, the orator who is wise does not take too much pains to hedge his statements and position at all points, but speaks broadly and boldly, regardless of exceptions which may be taken, and of variations from general truths for which he has no time to make provision. He leaves them to those whom they most concern.

Next to plain English, as tributary to perspicuity, comes what is called figurative speech.

Figures for clearness. It has several uses, but the element in it wanted for lucidity is based upon comparison of the less known with the well known, of the obscure with the familiar. There are various opinions in regard to the use of comparisons, but the listener who does not clearly apprehend the meaning of a speaker is usually grateful for the light which comes from a well-chosen simile or metaphor.

It is not always remembered that the figures of comparison are allied to the highest function *The compara- tive faculty.* of the mind, the elaborative or discursive faculty—the faculty of relations whose exercise results in analysis and synthesis. For if the mind affirms one thing of another it joins them in synthesis; if it denies one thing of another it separates them in analysis. Judgment itself is the comparison of two notions directly, and reasoning is the comparison of two terms with each other through a third, and thus various forms of thought are manifestations of the working of the faculty of comparison. Accordingly, whenever a figure of comparison is used the mind is working in the line of its main activity. What makes it seem to be out of its usual course and a turning aside from it, a trope, is because the skilful and pleasing comparison consists in finding the identity which exists in things apparently unlike in many respects. Ajax and the lion resemble each other in boldness only, but its prominence in the beast emphasizes the same quality in the man by being made equal or identical. The Scipios and thunderbolts are alike in the destructive quality only; but the death-dealing element in the men is better understood by identification with lightning.

The one essential for clearness in all comparison is, that what may be called the illuminating term be perfectly understood by the hearer, and that it contain a point of identity, with the term to be illustrated, or at least of similarity to it. For example, to most persons ten years ago it would not have added to clearness of statement if it had been said, that Macaulay's style is as diaphanous as if it were pervaded by the cathode ray, while to affirm that it is as clear as daylight is to identify it in respect of perspicuousness with what everybody accepts as a common symbol of transparency. Upon this feature of their familiarity rests the marvellous fitness of the similitudes in the gospel parables of the kingdom. They are all from the common stock of daily sights and sounds, occupations and emotions of human life; but they throw light upon spiritual truths which were obscure to a generation that was slow of understanding.

It is sometimes asked how this faculty of comparison can be acquired. One is tempted to answer: As the gift of imagination or of versifying, of computing or of reasoning, or any other inborn power is acquired. But after all it may be more of a matter of cultivation than of inheritance.

When it is remembered that our language is a vast fabric of fossil metaphors, over which we trip as unconsciously as a child over the coal measures beneath the turf, it would seem that the comparative faculty belongs in a measure to everybody. Making all allowance for imitation in speech, the constant use of comparison for illustration or emphasis indicates how almost universal this power is, and that in some degree it belongs to all who think and speak. But the difference in degree also shows that diversity in gift and in cultivation is also vast. Much may be done by search for similarity in things unlike, by inquiring of every object in nature what immaterial truth it typifies, and of every transaction in human life what spiritual process it symbolizes. If these similarities and partial identities should then be stored away as carefully as the ancients laid aside and labelled their commonplaces and their *topica* for future use, or even as our modern Emerson posted in note-books his day's increment of thought to be torn out and used when he needed it,—if such pains were taken with the fruits of comparison they might be available when wanted. The habit of looking for identical points in things unlike would be cultivated, which after all is the main object of exercising this faculty. Of course its free and certain action in composition, or in the stimulating moment of extemporaneous speech is a most desirable end to be obtained.

None will be more ready, however, to admit the dangers which beset the comparative faculty than those who possess it in a remarkable degree. A great preacher of the last generation used to say, that in the midst of fervid extemporary discourse, all heaven and earth and things under the earth crowded images upon his imagination. Out of such a motley troop it must have been difficult to choose the single metaphor that was both pertinent and also in good taste. Indeed there is evidence that this last quality is often sacrificed to the first one, and the dignity of the subject is impaired by the inferiority of the thing with which it is associated. There may occasionally be a necessity for this degrading process, as when Milton likens the fallen archangel Satan to a "toad squat by the ear of

Eve" in the character of a seducing tempter. Contrast this with the exalting similitude with which the poet portrays his nobility as a prince of heaven, towering "like Atlas or Teneriffe." Nowhere more than in the use of figurative language is there need to observe carefully the law of eternal fitness. Its range is both high and low, but woe to him who does not distinguish between similes which make clear, and those which degrade a noble thought, or dignify an ignoble one. It were better that he use plain language, and trust to the hearer's good sense, than cause the inevitable discord which the listener will instinctively feel between the two things compared, if they are not in the same plane. The man who illustrated the right to find and assimilate other people's ideas was more effective than elegant when he remarked, " I eat turkey: I do not turn into turkey, the turkey turns into me." This is good enough for plagiarism, but somewhat below the grade of that process by which thoughts are gathered and assimilated as Chaucer and Shakespeare would have conducted the operation. Still, perhaps, it is as apt a resemblance as can be found to illustrate assimilation as distinguished from appropriation.

The minting of new coin out of old, stamping it with a new image and superscription; and out of discarded materials the manufacture of new paper, bearing the transformer's own water-mark, are other illustrations of mental assimilating processes. In these comparisons the mixed character of the original material and the high excellence of the final product exhibit a growth toward perfection which saves the degradation of the first part from appearing in the last, and leaves an agreeable impression in the end.

Thus far the figure of speech has been considered as an aid to perspicuity. It has other uses which may be explained in their proper place; but its first use and chief value is to throw light upon the less known by reflection from the well known, as the nature of the spiritual and immaterial kingdom of truth is made plain in the Bible by comparisons with the kingdoms of nature and life, with which every one is familiar. The good life, like the good tree, is known by its fruit. The power of a germ-truth is like the ferment of yeast. The implanting of evil among the good, like tares sown while men slept. Wisdom is like a treasure hid in a field, to be bought at any cost. Seeing the truth in the familiar instance, the hearer admits it in the unfamiliar as soon as the point of identity which exists between them is shown.

The chief caution to be observed in the use of illustrative figures for clearness is, that they should be employed only when obscurity or abstruseness of thought requires them. They should never be used to explain obscurity of language, when the same pains that are taken to find an illustration would make expression plain and clear by appropriate words properly arranged.

III.

ENERGY.

A SPEAKER'S expression of his thought should always be readily intelligible, but at times it should have added to its perspicuity a quality which has been called by many names since Aristotle termed it Energy. Force, strength, vigor, vivacity, power, have represented so many different notions of what an oration should have besides clearness. Some of these terms, the lexicographers will say, belong only to the mind and not to its product, while others denote partial activity; but in spite of verbal, distinctions it is possible that the Stagirite's *energeia—action*, as distinguished from *exis—habit*, more nearly represents what the orator must add to perspicuity, if he would be effective. For while the habitual speech must be clear, the occasional action in it will be energetic and emphatic. If this last word were not usually restricted to syllables, words, and single sentences, it would express more nearly than any other the stress which is placed upon the more important passages of an oration. There is, of course, the energetic habit of any orator who rises above the monotony of didactic lecturing; but higher than this upper level should rise at times the forceful assertion and the irresistible appeal which mark the highest attainment of speech. It will be designated here by one and another of the above-mentioned names, but the quality itself will be readily understood by all who have recognized it in the true orator as emphatic.

It will be admitted that the general tone of an oration should be energetic as distinguished from didactic moderation. Even the information which is conveyed by nar- **Pervasive energy.** rative and exposition will not be in the style of a historical or scientific lecture. It will have an interest and a movement which will compel attention, such as is given to a lecturer often by constraint. On the other hand, the speaker will not give all his strength to narration, exposition, or even to argumentation. Vivacity, rapidity, and solidity will be in place here, lending variety to delivery, and affording relief to the hearer ; but emphatic energy will be reserved for its own occasional stages in the progress of discourse. What and where these stages are, will be determined by the nature of the oration and the good sense of the speaker. In general it may be said, that they will be at the close of each main division if, as it ought, the treatment of the several topics is climacteric. Moreover, the same law of climax will prevail in the succession of emphatic utterances until the end of the discourse is reached, and the final and strongest paragraph is pronounced in the peroration.

Such occasional emphasis also contributes variety to discourse. If a continuous energy is put forth the effect will be a monotony as tiresome as a uniform indifference of manner. For this reason it has been sometimes recommended that the speaker do not try to do his best in every passage, but purposely drop to a lower level in places. A

Emphasis.

better suggestion is that he secure variety by carefully diversifying his composition, bestowing as much pains upon subordinate portions to make them interesting as upon the higher flights to make them effective. Variety does not necessitate inferiority. The very fervor of the emphatic passage may hide defects which would be apparent in moderate discourse. It was one of the maxims of a certain popular lecturer that poverty of thought could sometimes be compensated by energy of delivery. As a rule, however, he did not attempt to make a dead level of his utterances by filling the valleys with noise, any more than by bringing the mountain-tops low with indifferent elocution. The true orator sees the same necessity of diversity in speech as in the landscape, if he would excite interest and retain the attention of his hearers. An occasional emphasis of energy, then, being admitted, the methods of putting it forth may profitably be considered.

With the speaker, as distinguished from the writer, his manner will be the main exponent of energy and emphasis. *Personal force.* Where the writer must rely upon words and their arrangement, the earnest orator can give intensity to simple, or even ineffective, diction by stress of voice. The truth of this is often exemplified in the report of a speech into which the speaker threw his whole soul in delivery but whose words in print move no one. Much of the oratory which tradition has clothed with great celebrity has lost the power in print that it had on the lips of eloquence incarnate. The philippics no longer fulmine; the record of the apostolic sermon does not convert thousands; the printed reply to Hayne does not hold listeners breathless when it is read. The energy which is action, divine and godlike, is gone. Its absence is as painfully evident as its presence was once powerfully felt. It may read well, in spite of the old dictum, but it was better spoken, a hundred times better. Therefore the energy which is most effective in an oration will be that of the living, speaking man, in his voice and gesture, and in that earnestness of personal conviction and feeling which produce their counterpart in others. No better definition of such energy has ever been given than in Webster's famous characterization of true eloquence in his eulogy upon Adams and Jefferson. Every orator who would move an audience should have it by heart. Without the qualities there specified "labor and learning are in vain." With them, as primary conditions of effective speech, are associated certain tributary factors which add much to effectiveness. The natural orator is none the less efficient for being also a trained writer. Simple speech vigorously uttered is not of necessity as availing as skilled diction pronounced with equal energy. Accordingly the speaker will rely somewhat upon the words he uses as well as upon the emphasis he gives to important passages of his discourse.

For forcing a truth upon the average English-speaking hearer no diction can compare with the Anglo-Saxon, provided *Strong words.* that the thought be not philosophical, scientific, or abstruse. If it is, there will be no call for it in demonstrative oratory, which moves upon planes of common sense, and deals with ordinary men and facts, motives and principles. On such levels the language of everyday life affords the most unobstructed channel

for the communication of ideas.   No one mis-
understands it or has to think twice to comprehend it.   It conveys the thought without
diverting attention to the messenger.   It does
this instantly.   Great strength lies in its words.
They were born of a strong race ; used by
fighting men, hardy explorers, doughty con-
querors, enterprising settlers.   Their words
stood for deeds rather than thoughts, for feeling more than for contemplation.   Therefore
they are eminently useful in stirring those emotions which, more than thoughts, determine
the language of the orator whose purpose is to
evoke impulses in others which shall end in
right action.   For it is the immediate effect
that he is seeking, and directness in language is
a principal means to this end.   When he is
most in earnest and most energetic he will use
them most.   He will not employ the word
"conflagration" when his house is afire, nor
"arrest" to stop the thief running down the
street.   In like manner the speaker who wishes
his hearers to give their money, their
Plain speech.   influence, efforts, or themselves to
help the cause which he is advocating will not

"solicit contributions." If he desires to impress them profoundly and permanently with the lesson of a character or occasion he will not "recommend a favorable consideration of the instruction afforded by the subject we have been contemplating." He will find shorter and stronger words than these—words that strike straight to the head and heart, stir the soul and start the will.

Not that there is no use for the more deliberate and lingering word at times. Not every man or every audience can all at once be roused. There is a deliber- **Romance words.** ate energy and force in the slower movement of the Romance derivatives, which like laggard tides carry their meaning slowly but surely, so slowly that they make time for the sluggish mind to apprehend the drift of thought as they roll leisurely along. They are doing their work in bringing reflection and conviction gradually up to the point of resolution and action. But when that is reached the time has come for short, strong, and forceful words; and the speaker will go back for them to his old home in the North fast by the fountains of Urd and

Mimer, of judgment and of wisdom, on the shores of the Viking seas.

In obedience to a kindred law he will also employ the specific word for the general term when he needs to enforce a thought. The first thought is usually individual and specific.   It certainly is with the child, and with races in their childhood.   To the boy the elm is the tree which overhangs his home ; the genus *Ulmus* is his later generalization, but his quick thought is always of the ancestral roof-tree.   Nor does he ever get so old and philosophic that his mind is not distracted in its action when it attempts to include all the individuals of a class in one conception.   It is only a limited, indefinite number at best that he can bring together and hold in mind; and their composite image is more or less confused.   On the other hand, the essential representation of the entire class is better afforded by any single member of it, accidental differences being unimportant.   Accordingly the orator who wishes to make a strong impression in regard to the value of reformers, for example, will instance the work of Martin Luther rather than all the achievements of the whole class. He will name Napoleon for generalship, Washington for patriotism, Lincoln for all liberators of the oppressed. Always, too, the concrete will stand for the abstract, the particular for the general. It is the single point that penetrates and not the broad surface. Even water is not much impressed by a flat stroke. So the things by which the hearer is struck and which he retains are the definite points rather than the broad generalities and abstractions, which it is much easier to make than to find their concrete embodiment.

To this topic belongs the use of certain figures for emphasis, notably those which put for the whole of an object or a class a part of it or its associations. The *Figures for emphasis.* purse for wealth, gray hairs for age, the bench and the bar for judges and advocates, a sail for a ship, a sword for war, the pen for literature, the city for its inhabitants, marble for a statue, and canvas for a portrait, Homer for epic poetry, Hampden for heroism,—all these are more impressive than the names of the classes to which they belong. It would seem easier to pitch upon the part at once than to mention the whole. It is not. Generalization becomes the habit of advancing years, and the return to the specific is going back to one of the gifts of childhood, poetic and imaginative, which is sometimes lost through lack of use. There is a kingdom of truth and power into which the mind cannot enter except it become in one respect as a little child. The rhetorical interrogation, exclamation, hyperbole, apostrophe, antithesis, and epigram are figures which are impressive, but in proportion as they are sparingly employed. When the thought borders upon the inconceivable nothing can be better than the exclamatory "how" which no man can adequately answer. "How momentous this hour! how tremendous in its consequences!" But because the orator's business is to deal with ordinary events, and for the reason that extraordinary ones are rare and should have hyperbolical phrases reserved for them and them alone, he will be frugal in his use of these. In close combat with a debatable opinion the interrogative challenge to his hearers to deny his proposition if they can is a strongly emphatic mode of assertion, and lends variety and animation to discourse. The speaker should always be sure however of the consent of his audience to keep silence, every one of them, and not make an unexpected and confusing reply, taking his challenge too literally. Amusing and embarrassing examples are on record of too great presumption in this direction.

Perhaps the figure best suited to give emphatic force to a thought is the climax. Beginning with precise and perspicuous statement addressed to the under-

Climax.

standing of the hearer, the speaker will bring it within the circle of the sensibilities and emotions, employing those words which reach heart and soul, strengthening the expression and deepening the impression, and quickening the onward movement of discourse until it shall culminate in the best and strongest he can command. Such periodic energy, occurring not too often, but closing each important division, has a cumulative force greater than any sudden word however incisive, or brief phrase however brilliant. It is rather a steady gathering of power, as a billow gathers it, to hurl the fulness of its might upon the shore. Such emphasis, accumulated at proper intervals, comports with the measured dignity of oratorical movement, distinguished as it always should be from the more versatile progress of the essay with its scintillations and pleasant surprises. The climax of all preceding climaxes will occur, of course, in the peroration, which should leave the weight of the entire discourse upon the mind and heart of the hearer. It will be by a skilful disposition of emphasis, energy, and force that this is done. Points are all that the speaker has a right to expect will be remembered or recalled. Pages will be forgotten; but if he has drawn them into concluding points, and forced these into minds and hearts, he will have accomplished all that can be demanded of " winged words." Their power is in the energy and personality of him who speeds them like arrows from the bow of the mighty. It is an instantaneous power, evanescent, or living in fading memory. In either case, that which is most impressive, or best recalled, will be whatever was most strenuously enforced. As was remarked above, an appreciation of the value of becoming and discriminating delivery is essential to a right use of energy and emphasis. This belongs to another branch of the subject to be considered by itself. There must, however, be something to emphasize and enforce, else oratory becomes declamation, a discourse, dull and monotonous, or senseless with sound and fury. Accordingly the energetic thought of the speaker must precede his forcible and emphatic expression.

There is one phase of energy which is not always given the credit that belongs to it, namely, its reserves. By this is not meant a lack of force, or even the failure to put it forth when its possession is evident. It is rather the restraint of power somewhat within its utmost limit. It is typified by the powerful engine which does its work with apparent ease, without strain or jar, and is manifestly able to do much more at high pressure. There have been speakers who conveyed a similar impression. They were speaking magnificently, but with apparent ease, without straining or ranting, perhaps without flights of oratory, while the hearers waited for the burst of eloquence which they knew was possible. Such reserve may or may not be satisfactory ; but, all in all, it is preferable to the extreme endeavor which indicates that the orator has reached his highest point and can go no farther without collapse. It may be constantly wished that the speaker would do his best here and there, but his restraint may after all be more satisfactory than another man's boisterous rant. The listener never knows how much is reserved ; on the other hand he sometimes would like to know what might be done at the speaker's best. The subject is a rare one, and the occasion also when an orator may not find places to exert his utmost power once or twice in the course of his address. The audience is better pleased when they have had at least a glimpse of his highest attainment. Still, restraint is better than extravagance. Those writers who have made eloquence a virtue place on a par with temperance and self-control the force of will which prevents the oration from running into an abstract essay on the one hand, or on the other into "an over-ornamented prose-poem." To govern a logical propensity, or to restrain a flighty imagination, or to curb an impulse to rodomontade may require as much moral force as to suppress the appetite for any other sort of intoxication. It is the same here as in the exercise of all power; it must be done discreetly, fittingly, and with nice adjustment to the immediate need. Otherwise it becomes ridiculous in its over exercise, or inefficient in its failure.

A kindred form of reserve is the understatement of a case, which goes with the spirit of moderation and fairness. There *Moderation in statement.* would appear to be nothing emphatic about it, but it nevertheless sometimes helps the speaker's cause more than violent insistence upon its last claim. By leaving hearers to make a stronger case for him than he has urged, is a generosity which is likely to have its reward, especially if it take the form of fairness toward opposing considerations or persons. If suggestion goes half-way there is little need of exhausting the reserves of language, not to say of forestalling the inductive processes of hearers, by making the last demand, for they will supply what has not been said in their

sense of justice and fair play. Sometimes in
their bountifulness they will accord more to
the speaker than he would have asked at the
utmost. In such an event, and in every case,
the emphasis which an audience can give to
his moderate statement far outweighs any
vehement and extreme assertion that he himself might make. It is the world with Athan-
asius instead of against him.

IV.

ELEGANCE.

ORAL discourse should always be easily and readily apprehended ; sometimes it should be forcible in its presentation of emphatic phases of its subject ; it may furthermore gratify a love of excel- lence in literary art which most in- telligent hearers possess. Indeed, it would be difficult to find a person willing to listen at all to a speech of an hour in length who does not instinctively know the difference between elegance and uncouthness. He may not be able to say precisely in what this difference consists, but he will recognize it, and have his own way of stating his impression. There are compositions, especially of a poetic nature, both in verse and prose, where beauty of diction and wealth of imagery are of the first consequence.

They are essential to that æsthetic pleasure
which is the purpose of such composition.
But a serious and earnest speech, having a
definite object to secure in determining conviction, belief, or action, will seek the quality
of elegance so far only as it will contribute to
the purpose of the orator. This purpose being
different in character and in importance at different times, the degree of elegance sought
should vary correspondingly ; and while there
may be occasions too momentous for much of
it, there will be other occasions when this
feature of discourse will be both appropriate
and essential. At such times the speaker will
ask himself, In what does elegance of composition consist?

His answer will place it, chiefly, in a general
elevation of tone comporting with the dignity
of public address upon a topic which
will of necessity itself be dignified
by reason of the occasion and of the
character of the audience. Unconsciously he
will give a corresponding elevation to all that
is uttered. Not in stilted and bombastic phrase,
but with such sustained diction as exalted

Elevation of tone in dis-course.

sentiments require. It is in this adaptation of words and sentences to thoughts that elegance must primarily consist. Without such harmony of correspondence an oration might become a vulgar harangue. Furthermore, this fitness of diction to dignified thought must pervade the entire discourse in all its variety of expression, the humorous as well as the pathetic portions, the narrative as well as the argumentative. It will be like the elegance of a costly house, in its foundation and its walls, in its appointments and its adornments.

In what particulars this general atmosphere of elegance is to be carried out becomes a question of varied application. As all discourse is made up of words and *Appropriate diction.* their combination, the first recommendation must be in regard to the kind of words to be used, and also as to the way they are arranged. For every object in the material and immaterial world there are at least two names, one of honor and one of dishonor; for every act a verb which exalts or degrades. In poetry the first class of words is used, and dignified prose should employ a style of its own not inferior.

The best word is none too good, since language must always lag behind thought and report it imperfectly. Among the multitude of words, as among throngs of men, there are princes by nature and by suffrage, and no decree can make even their brethren equal to them in honor or in worth. " Man " will always be the highest title of a human being, whatever be the qualifying prefix or added limitation—as nobleman, gentleman, king or general, priest or poet; for manhood is greater than any sphere of its activity. So of every state and order of creation; there is the highest stage and the corresponding word, instead of which no inferior term is admissible in public speech, however endurable it may be in colloquial parlance, dramatic composition, or familiar correspondence.

As with words, so with their arrangement in sentences. The best of them may be so unnaturally ordered as to lose half their value. The strong or sonorous word may be weakened or smothered by its inferiors, and these in turn may gain nothing by promotion. The laws of rhythm may

be violated and the resonance of a period destroyed by the misplacing of a syllable. This,
of course, is no fatal mistake in the direction of
clearness or force, but if elegance is worth seeking at all it should be sought diligently. Not
as mere ornament, but as an essential part of
harmonious construction for the gratification of
an artistic sense when this is permissible and
commendable. On the contrary the accidental
or deliberate introduction of words that jar
upon the ear can have for its apology one or
two reasons only: an intentional discord in the
thought, to which expression is to correspond;
or a harshness of sound designed to serve as a
relief to long-sustained harmony. But the
harmony itself ought not to be of the kind, nor
to be continued so long, as to need a contrasting crash to awaken hearers from its drowsy influences.

The use of imagery for elegance may be
mentioned here. The creations of the imagination are as welcome to the hearer as Imagery for
to the reader, and as effective in the beauty.
oration as in the poem. The delight of dis-
covering the connection between suggested

similitudes gives the listener a share in the speaker's creative processes, besides stimulating his attention and arousing his mental activities. Sometimes he is started on new and kindred lines of thought by a passage which has stirred him by its beauty. Again, his admiration is won by the power which discerns resemblances in things remote from each other, and apparently incongruous. It is akin to the pleasure which comes from the unexpected in music and painting and sculpture.

Elegance, however, can never be a matter of words, sentences, and figures of speech alone. **Fitness in thought.** Underneath the best expression must always lie the beautiful thought, as the inner glory of life is behind every outer manifestation of its excellence. No choice expression can gild an ugly fact, as no euphemism can make disease, or death, or crime, a welcome contemplation. On the other hand, if the thought be full of health, and life, and innocence, it will carry the beauty and gladness of these into almost any word that can suggest them. Moreover, there is a great wealth of words for the things which bring joy into human life and peace into human hearts and prosperity to communities. When, therefore, a speaker is discoursing on such topics as make for justice and honor, and through these happiness, he will find the beauty which inheres in his subject growing out into visible forms by the law of a life which cannot be restrained. It will take on its own form and color according to the mind out of which it is springing, as flowers take their hues from the soil and the clime in which they grow. If, united with these natural tastes, there be also a perception of the harmonies of proportion and rhythm, of fitness between sound and sense, of correspondence between subject and style, between the speaker and his topic, of concord between the occasion and the orator, and of the sympathy which the audience should have with both, the product in speech cannot be inelegant any more than it can fail to be forcible and clear.

V.

ADAPTATION.

TO the preceding triad of essentials in public discourse should be added a fourth, which is so comprehensive that it may include not only these qualities but other and minor excel-

Adaptation a far-reaching principle. lences discussed at length in books upon composition. If but a single maxim were to be given to the begin-ner, or even the adept in oratory, it should be concerning the fitness of things. A trite phrase speaks of this as "eternal," but the word is not too strong in its expression of an ultimate and universal truth. Exemplifications of it are everywhere apparent in the world of animate being. It is only in unnatural, artificial, and perverted conditions that this law of adapta-tion of means to end, of life to its environ-ment, of creature to the purpose of its creation is violated. In that department of action which is known as the communication of thought in oral address from man to man, from mind to mind, there is unceasing opportunity to fulfil the requirements of this law. Unfortunately there is equal opportunity to transgress it, as is sometimes seen when a number of speakers address the same assembly. Some will observe the unities and proprieties and some will not. Or with both classes there will be a partial success and a partial failure, notably in the speeches, more or less extemporaneous and ill-considered, which follow banquets. But in the carefully written oration the law of adaptation should be the golden rule of the writer: to count those things important which make for harmony.

This is a fundamental principle of every kind of composition. It belongs to the poem and the essay, to the historical work and the mathematical treatise, to the digest of laws and the romantic story. To interchange the style of one with another would be like placing the novelist on the bench, and setting the mathematician to write poetry.

The laws of necessity and common sense permit no such harlequinade in everyday affairs, and in literature such buffoonery is as short-lived as it is amusing.   Meantime each department has its own proprieties to which any of its performances are held, and by which they are judged. None are more exposed to this canon of criticism than the oral address.   Any discords are sure to be detected by some listener, who directly becomes the centre from which contagious and rapidly spreading judgment proceeds.   Counter currents may meet it, but they as often will be full of added criticism about other discords as denials of the first fault.   It does not require an eminent development of acumen to discover an incongruity.   Often the hearer cannot give the reason for what he has felt, as he cannot expose a fallacy in argument of which he is sensible.   But the discord has jarred upon some auditory nerve, or upon some æsthetic, moral, or religious sensibility. He cannot define or explain it better than he can describe the discord which grated upon his ear out of the tumult of a symphony.   Yet he has felt it, and it cannot be beaten out of him

by saying that the discord is a part of the harmony. Such are the judges which have sat
upon oratory since one of the people began to
speak to all the people.

Therefore the speaking man, as the ancients
called him, has great need of studying the harmonies of thought and subject, of
time and place, of the audience and
his own attitude toward them. His
judge is the multitude, many-minded, many-
eared, many-tongued. What escapes one will
be caught by his neighbor, and the third or
tenth man will detect what eluded the two or
nine. And the two and nine will hear of it and
tell of it as their own discovery, through sheer
mortification that they were not the original
detectors. On the other hand it should be
said just here, that commendation is no less
contagious, and that an audience is often more
ready to praise a good point than to condemn
a bad one. Applause is more frequent than
hisses, even in a political convention. So, also,
the sense of what is in good taste and what in
poor is always inherent in the collective humanity which is assembled to listen to what

one of its individuals has to say. Its agreement with him or its dissent will, in nine cases out of ten, be traced to his observance of fitnesses or to his disregard and violation of them. What are some of the directions in which danger lies?

The most obvious, though not the most frequent source of discord, is the unsuitableness of a subject to an audience. This occurs when some topic is introduced which they had no reason to expect. *Unsuitableness of subject.* There is always a kind of unwritten agreement between a speaker and his hearers that the general subject of discussion shall not be offensive and that it shall be of common interest. If this understanding is violated listeners will take their revenge in ways too well known to need enumerating. Nor will they put themselves in the way of a second surprise.

A similar danger lies in discussing matters unsuited to the occasion. This is the temptation lying in wait for those who once a week, and year after year, are expected to present something fresh and new, or the old truth in a new and attractive form, to their Sunday congregations. When the address is out of the usual line its occasional character is sometimes urged as an apology for an excursiveness in theme which has an element of unexpectedness in it, striking the hearers as incongruous and out of place. The same is true of an absurd or sensational treatment of a well-worn topic. The interest which novelty excites is more than neutralized by the ridiculous blending of the solemn with the ludicrous. A like revulsion of feeling follows any incompatibility between a topic and its treatment. Such discussion jars upon that sense of fitness which is a part of men's common sense. If this be lacking to the person who happens to be the speaker, and to a few sympathizers before him, it is not wanting to the aggregate of his hearers. The average taste of a well-informed audience is not far removed from the best standards of criticism.

In this treatment of a theme the speaker will also see to it that his diction corresponds to the character of his subject. As this is commonly dignified, his language will not be too colloquial, common-place, trivial, or diverting. People do not

Correspondence of diction and theme.

come together in these days for this sort of amusement. They can be entertained elsewhere. Here they expect what is becoming. Grave questions that are always arising in a republic are not topics to be discussed in the language of the club and the saloon. Dignified conversation may be the ideal of the speaker in some situations, but he will remember that his partner is a multitude and its voice, as of many waters, expressing many minds if it could be allowed. Some respect is due to numbers, and he will unconsciously give to his address an elevation correspondingly dignified, if he is a man of right instincts. At the same time he will assume no cringing attitude by reason of the great throng before him. It is after all an assemblage of units. It has no higher intellectual level than that of the ablest person in it, except in wider information. Addressing this one, the speaker has nothing greater to fear. Mind cannot be multiplied by hundreds and thus be made colossal, and the orator has no reason in the nature of things to fear a thousand more than he would the best man of the thousand. Much stage fright would be banished if young speakers could bear this in mind, while genuine respect might often be increased. For, strangely enough, a speaker will boldly utter sentiments to a mixed multitude that he would be slow to announce in conversation with some eminent person whom he discovers in its ranks. His consolation and encouragement is that he is talking to the average hearer. It is also safer to address the best intellect in language which this average hearer can comprehend.

In this instance of adaptation certain suggestions about style will be in place. Simplicity, for example, is not inconsistent with *Simplicity of style.* the dignity that has been mentioned. Clear, straightforward sentences are desirable, out of which parenthetic thoughts have been weeded. These may be transplanted as separate propositions in distinct sentences if worth keeping and enlarging. Short sentences also are easier retained than long ones, and loose are understood more immediately than periodic. These last have an advantage, however, in retaining attention to their close, and thus cultivating the habit of listening—a habit and a

power which is being lost by this much-read-
ing, impatient generation.   Attention, like
memory, is becoming one of the lost arts, a
gift and a talent which died with the fathers
and went out with the hourglass.   The long
sentence, also, provided it is clear, as it may
be, carries a weight of accumulated energy in
its culminating forms that cannot be dispensed
with in the climaxes of eloquence.

There is one element which this practical age
is trying to eliminate from oratory in order to
The dramatic element. bring it into correspondence with its
own hard-and-fast theories.   Or, per-
haps, taking its cue from the British Parliament, as it gets other fashions from across the
water, it attempts to lower the standards of
genuine eloquence, as they have been lowered
to business talk in that body where the deliberative oratory of the eighteenth century
survives only in tradition, or in exceptional
instances so notable as to need no mention.
Through fear of being considered dramatic, an
essential part of the best speaking is condemned to exile by legislators; and in this condemnation the highest attainments of the best

orators the world has known, are incidentally or impliedly included, and their influence on succeeding oratory deprecated. A slight knowledge of those periods when the drama has been succeeded by genuine eloquence ought to show the fallacy and the folly of such objections. It was the dramatic spirit passing into the oratory of the Greek play before the speech abandoned the drama—the spirit which it took with itself later into the courts and the agora—that gave the eloquence of Hellas its power. The same gift was conferred by the French drama upon the orators of the golden age of Louis Fourteenth; and the Elizabethan dramatists, together with Hellenic studies, did as much for the giants of the Hanoverian Parliament in the last century. In general it may be asserted, that in any age where oratory has risen above the discussions of the board of trade, the dramatic element has been present with its own incomparable power. This is by no means saying that an orator must be an actor in the common acceptation of the term. But he must have what Demosthenes called the first, second, and third requisite of eloquence—*ac-*

tion, in its proper degree resembling the energy
and appropriate activity of the dramatic interpreter and impersonator.   Other things being
equal, the more of the dramatic spirit that inspires a speaker the more effective will he be.
Such a spirit will compel the speaker to give
his utmost expression to thought, knowing as
he must that he cannot fully represent any idea
in all its possibilities by words alone.   The eye
sees more than the ear hears.   Therefore it
also must be addressed.   But the dramatic
forms of language, the interrogations, the rare
exclamation, the reply, the appeal, the affirma-
tion, and the denial are all tokens and out-
growths of that spirit of action and animation
without which oratory becomes the dullest of
recitative.   Therefore the dramatic spirit should
be cultivated; for it will be in accord with the
best eloquence, and will lend something to the
most commonplace utterances.   Like a good
manner in other things, it is everything to
some people and something to everybody.   It
is more to the insensible than they can be conscious of, and for this reason should be encour-
aged.   One thing is certain, true eloquence

will never be attained by studying restraint, by suppressing the natural exuberance of youthful enthusiasm, and by imitating models of dull and prosy uniformity. Men in the next generation will not be moved by orators who, with hands in pockets, mutter, in monotone, sentiments that may be apples of gold, but are offered in baskets of silver.

Besides the forms of adaptation thus far mentioned, there is another not less important of which a speaker might seem to need no reminder, namely, congruity **Naturalness and imitation.** between his subject, his audience, his oratorical methods, and himself. In other words he is to adapt himself to these in his own way, to cultivate naturalness and bide the result. If he succeeds it will be because he has been true to himself; if he fails it will not be because he neglected to imitate some greater orator. This orator did not make himself famous by imitation of one greater still. Whatever of distinction he has, represents the difference between himself and all others. It is his own individuality improved and raised to the highest power. So, in its own degree, must the personality of

12

every speaker be his own key to success.   The
secret of cultivating one's originality is the absence of self-consciousness, which is secured by
profound absorption in the subject.   One may
greatly admire another man's way of discussing
an interesting question in a heated debate, or
of managing a dispute which comes perilously
near to blows; but when he himself is in the
quarrel he will conduct it in his own way,
good or poor.   There is no self-consciousness
then.   His style is his own and has no affec-
tation in it.   But the same man will sit down
to compose a speech, perhaps on the very issue
about which he has been hotly contentious, and
will begin to think how Webster, or Sumner,
or Phillips would have treated the matter, and
forthwith he attempts to adopt the methods of
one of these, or possibly of all three at once.
The attempt is the limit of his execution.
Clever parodies of verse and travesties of prose
have been made which preserve the caricature
which makes one laugh, but unfortunately
serious imitation has the same effect, though
undesigned.   In so far as the speaker follows
the proclivity of the ape he obtains the ape's

reward of laughter at his grave and serious mimicry. With this tribute also goes the sentiment that he ought to know better, and be himself or be nobody. Better be a nonentity than a shadow. No man has arrived at the years of discretion who may not know, if he will, whether there is anything of his own worth cultivating. If there is, it is a waste of time and labor to import, or try to smuggle in, the manner of another. For after all it is nothing but the manner that can be copied. Abilities are inalienable possessions, and naught but their methods of exhibition can be appropriated. To clothe moderate capacities in the garments of genius suggests the single idea of misfit, of which the illustration is as old as the fable of the lion's skin from out whose shaggy terror proceeded nothing more terrific than a bray.

If, however, the speaker can determine to be natural, that is, to make the best of such capacities as he possesses in the largest degree, he will arrive the earlier at such eminence as is possible to him. Certain it is, he will not arrive by any other road. Moreover, it will be his easiest road;

for there is a bent and grain in every nature which it is easy to follow.   To cross it may be a waste of well-meant effort.   With the man of strong logical powers the ambition to excel in works of the imagination is commendable but unwise.   The poet may wish that reasons were as natural to him as rhyme, and still waste half a lifetime in studying syllogisms.   So an orator, naturally logical, may aspire to the emotional, or if sympathetic to the didactic, or if persuasive to the instructive.   His business is to discover the direction in which he can work most easily and naturally, and to go with the current of his nature.   It may not run parallel with his ideal orator's drift, but all the better if he cut a fresh channel.   Imagine Henry Clay trying to confine the broad floods of his eloquence within the deep defiles through which Webster's flowed and thundered.   Picture Abraham Lincoln in an endeavor to mould his rugged speech after the Greek models which Edward Everett brought from Athens.   What a figure the self-contained, and therefore mob-controlling, Phillips would have made if he had imitated the coruscating, impetuous Choate!

Fancy any one of these condescending to adapt methods not his own, or to cultivate any talents but those with which he was royally endowed. Each one instinctively knew which way the grain in his communicative nature ran, and he followed it freely, devotedly, and successfully. According to his ability, this is the condition of every speaker's success, so far as the manner of his working is concerned. Other and many requisites lie along his path, but this is the way in which he is to walk. His patient, solitary labor and his public effort are both in the one direction of his natural style, which Buffon aptly termed, " the man himself." Therefore in this department of life, as in every other, he will be himself.

No one of course will suppose that " being natural " signifies continuing in that state of nature which belongs to childhood and youth. This is the mistake of those who consider themselves or their friends " natural orators." In our present artificial systems of instruction much has to be changed to restore lost naturalness to the child of nature, who remains such from two to three years only according to surroundings. Charles Lamb asked in his time, " Is childhood dead ? " and it has been said in ours, that infancy and manhood are the two ages now remaining out of the original seven. Naturalness is the progressive attainment of a lifetime. It is training the growing faculty of speech, for example, to work in its best and freest way, untrammelled by the artificialities of primary instruction, and emancipated from the self-consciousness of subsequent years. It is the perfected nature of maturity, as distinguished from that of childhood; nature in cultivation, not running wild; the naturalness of the fruit-bearing tree, not of the wayside dwarf. This is not to be understood as overlooking the fact that there have been speakers who have moved multitudes by their native eloquence. The gift, like that of verse, is inborn and cannot be destroyed or repressed by lack of culture. On the other hand training and cultivation render such talents preeminently effective, to say nothing of calling forth and making useful moderate and sometimes unsuspected abilities.

To the attainment of naturalness the studies

of the orator should be constantly directed.
Formerly, and for centuries, all
study was pursued with this end
in view. *(marginal note: Liberal studies.)* Amidst the division and subdivision of curricula in the schools of the present
day, courses similar to the mediæval *trivium*
and *quadrivium*, or to the ancient order of
instruction, might be selected ; but for the
speaker, as for the physician, the architect,
or the engineer, and more even than for these,
a broad and comprehensive education is the
best preparation. There is no branch of literature, science, or philosophy that may not
contribute to the enlarged views which the
demonstrative orator should be able to take
upon occasion. Of all men he needs a worldwide acquaintance with things and men, with
facts and principles, with theories and laws.
And if, as a professional man, he is dealing
daily with the routine of his narrower duty, he
should at least know where the larger outlook
may be obtained, and what avenues open into
fields which he may need to explore upon demand. Possessed of this knowledge, he will
be able readily to meet such demand with the

naturalness with which a busy man turns aside from his vocation to an avocation, from trade or manufacture to a question of literature or good government, bringing into the discussion the results of a large and instructive experience.

VI.

PERSONAL AND ETHICAL QUALITIES.

TO give directions that would be satisfactory to every writer is as impossible as to say how history or biography, a novel or a poem, is to be written. All good work is a creation and a growth, as difficult to order as the upspringing of a twig and the subsequent expansion of the tree. Thought processes and word-choosing are innate gifts, which much practice develops, but never bestows. To cultivate thoughtfulness, observation, and reflection, to study the words, sentences, and paragraphs of the best stylists, does much for the original power of thought and expression where it exists. But it must be possessed in some encouraging degree. If it is, it will generally

Nature and art in composition.

manifest itself in both the ability and desire to compose. If to these be joined the disposition and habit of natural and free communication, the way is open to success for the speaker who has anything worth telling. Still, it is not to be denied, that beyond natural gifts and graces, which will find an outlet in their own way, there are particular methods that belong to certain classes of composition, the oration among them. It is well known that even the free spirit of poetry is not beyond the assistance of the schools, and that the rambling pen of the essayist is helped by the suggestions of writers upon rhetoric. By all means, then, so organic and orderly a creation as the public address should not be entirely independent of recommendations, although it should be exempt from rules that fetter and hamper.

The qualities which are suggested in this chapter have a general character, belonging to what may be regarded as the atmosphere of demonstrative discourse, and are to be distinguished from the specific qualities already mentioned. The former are to the latter what the general bearing of the

General qualities.

speaker is to his particular methods of address and his personal characteristics of expression, as distinct from his words and oratorical action.   As preliminary to these general qualities it will be remembered that among the fundamental conditions of demonstrative speech were its unprofessional character; a clear understanding of the reason and purpose of speaking at all; the subject in relation to the object; the plan, introduction, discussion, and peroration.   To these elements of structure certain features of composition were added, tending to make for the ready comprehension, by his hearers, of the speaker's message, such as clearness and force.   These are enumerated to make more emphatic the statement that beyond them all are larger attributes of speech which cannot be overlooked when the best efficiency is to be sought, and the highest and most lasting success achieved.

With these observations in mind the reader should have some notion of the distinctive character of composition in occasional discourse.   He will not, as in poetry, make expression the main purpose,

Variety and breadth of treatment.

keeping the theme in comparative subordina-
tion, unless he intends to compose an epic.
Nor will he make information and instruction
through exposition the end of his effort, caring
little for the manner of conveying truth provided it is clearly stated and firmly lodged in
the hearer's understanding. Instead, he will
have need of first one and then another method,
as statement, exposition, or illustration may
be needed in the progress of his discourse.
At the same time the statement is not to be
that of a scientist elucidating the mysteries of
the siderial heavens or of the great deep, nor
of the lawyer setting forth his case to a jury, nor
will his illustrations be made the stock of a
page, as a poet might make them. Rather he
is to seize upon what is essential in these professional forms and the spirit of them to incorporate into the unprofessional and occasional
production, which is unlike any other. His
statement, therefore, will be clear and intelligible, but not too minute and prolix; his argument strong, but not too finely drawn; his
illustration a flashlight rather than the varie-
gated succession of rainbow tints from a re-

volving prism. This strength and breadth of treatment in the several kinds of composition which will inevitably be required in an oration as the most inclusive of all types of literature, will also be needed in matters of diction and style. In precision, for example, exactness will be sought, but not the nicety of the scientific writer who would write *larus* instead of sea-gull, and *goura* for pigeon. The popular terminology is sufficiently correct for address to the people on subjects which concern the populace. Such a habit of speech will also ensure that perspicuity without which eloquence is useless. Even in the energy of speaking there is opportunity to discriminate between an impetuous torrent and a varied flow like that of a stream which has its quiet reaches as well as its rapids and precipitous falls.

From these precepts, having a common basis, may be gathered the principle lying underneath them all, namely, that breadth and strength rather than minute accuracy, niceness, and fineness, should prevail in the oral treatment of a theme. This

does not imply or excuse inaccuracy and misrepresentation and error.   Painful precision is
better than these.   It has the merit of a wholesome respect for the truth, which itself always
commands respect.   In general, it may be said
that the handling of a subject before the people
should be with the broad and positive stroke
of the scene-painter rather than with the minute
pencilling of the miniature artist working upon
ivory.   But however strong the stroke designed
for immediate effect, there must be no faulty
drawing and impossible perspectives.   There
need be little artistic sense in an audience to
detect a slanting perpendicular, or an oval
where there should be a circle.   Hearers are
keen to discover obtuse or acute angles where
there should be right-angled statements, and
to find obliquities in a speaker's disposition
where they looked for fairness and integrity.
Fallacies and sophistries may pass for a while
and with one and another, but not forever and
with all.   Lincoln's aphorism will already have
risen to the reader's lips: " You can fool some
of the people all the time, all the people some
of the time, but not all the people all the time."

Accordingly the wise speaker will be upright and downright in the method of his speech, and also broad and strong in the manner of it. He will strike at centres, and let his critics take care of circumferences; at the roots and let the branches follow the fortunes of the roots.

There should also be the same definiteness in the structure of the discourse. The sections of it should be few, but distinct. A continuous monologue is unimpressive; so is minute and multitudinous division and subdivision. In neither method is there the possibility to make points that will be remembered. Two or three that can be recalled for a week are better than the twenty which are forgotten in an hour. Therefore the fabric of an oral address ought to be woven in broad bands of contrasting color, and not too many of them. The hearer will carry them in his memory as he cannot an intricate pattern. Such simplicity of design is a part of the force which should prevail everywhere, and also is in accord with the law of economizing the mental strain of the hearer. In this way he loses less of what has been offered him than if an elabo-rate mosaic had been traced for his comprehen-sion or confusion.

As a natural sequence to this strength and breadth of treatment, should follow the quality of elucidation. This is something more than clearness. It is possible to be perspicuous and yet leave the subject in a haze. Almost every topic is liable to mis-understanding, and much that is erroneous is mistaken for truth. What is needed by the orator in any case when confusion of right and wrong, the expedient and the inexpedient, may occur, is the power to clear the mists away, and to show things in their true relations. It is the larger exercise of perspicuity, and is to the re-vealing of affairs what right words are to the transmission of thought. How often does it happen in assemblies of men who are ostensibly seeking the same results, but differ in methods advocated, that each speaker adds new compli-cations, and increases the general confusion, begetting distrust and discouragement. At length some speaker with more open vision than the rest will send his clear, well-defined

conceptions over the turbulent throng, marking out the metes and bounds of the subject,
and straightway the drifting, shifting opinions
begin to find their own places, and to crystallize with mathematical regularity.   He has
said, "Let there be light," and there is light
in the chaos; the waters are divided and dry
land appears, and day is no longer as the night.
It was this elucidating power which made Pericles the commanding orator that he was.   Aris-
tophanes says of him, that "his eloquence
cleared the social atmosphere as thunder and
lightning, and stirred up all Greece."   He
brushed away sophisms, he made those things
important that were important, consigned the
subordinate to their proper place, and set forth
the real and proper relations of truth, justice
and liberty.   Such a power, joined with verbal
power, is the most effective and satisfactory
that a speaker can possess—to see the truth,
and to make others see it.   To acquire this
ability is among the possibilities of an ethical
education.   It implies freedom from inher-
ited or adopted prejudices, with the possession of dispassionate judgment, deliberate

13

consideration, and something of the prophet's vision beyond the veil of immediate surroundings. It is what every speaker should covet earnestly as one of the best gifts. His highest commendation will be that he makes things clear, that he reveals the truth, exposes error masquerading in the garb of truth, opens men's eyes to deceit, and lets them know on what ground they stand. Then if they go wrong they go with eyes open; and it cannot be said of him that he has been a blind leader of the blind because he would not take pains to see and to make them see also.

Such a revealing touch implies a third quality of effectiveness, which may be defined as the The finding power. power of finding and touching the moral sense of the hearer. It is one thing to talk about and around a topic, to look at it from a safe and comfortable distance, and another thing to make a listener feel that its practical lesson is not so much other men's business as his own. Unless this conviction prevails at the close of a speech, there has been a waste of time, or else mere entertainment. Immediate action may not be demanded, but immediate impulse should be communicated, and the reflective and reformative power set to work. It was said of one among a group of orators that he excelled the rest " because he left his sting in the minds of his hearers." The suggestion may not be so pleasant as it is expressive, but the speaker who does not leave a stimulating or inspiring thought in thoughtful minds has left out of his address another of its cardinal requisites.

Such a characteristic, however, requires another which pertains to the moral constitution, and that is courage. It is a remark- Courage of able topic and a singular audience convictions. where this quality will not be much needed before an orator has properly and thoroughly handled any theme which is worth bringing before the public on the platform in these busy days. He will find in such an assembly much independent thinking and some scepticism. But the last temper which any listener wishes to discover in a speaker is timidity, or fear, or doubt of his own position. The courage of his own convictions is essential to the beginning of communicating them to others. Besides this,

there is also a courageous way of doing it.   An
audience sometimes looks like an army in battle array against the man who is talking to it.
Sometimes it is such, silent, sullen, as much on
the defensive as if it were intrenched in pits
instead of chairs.   It is not respectful and
temporary silence that can give much boldness
to an orator who knows that the return fire is
only an hour distant, to be prolonged indefin-
itely.   His courage should be something that
will outlast the present moment.   Yet for
this moment he needs a good supply to face
the dissent, the prejudice, the antagonism, of
an opposing public sentiment.   The great triumphs of oratory have been in this courageous
enforcement of an unwelcome message, more
than in the voicing of the concordant and agree-
ing opinions of a multitude.   So Demosthenes
spoke to temporizing Athenians; so Phillips to
his fellow-citizens, standing by their cotton
trade; so Beecher to England, fearing its mills
would be closed in the cause of freedom.

Such are some of the essential conditions of
a speech that is to be effective.   They belong
to its general character, but they are not gen-

eral or indefinite in their own.   Lesser things may be overlooked, but the broad and strong lines of construction, clear and satisfactory elucidation of the perplexities that gather about most subjects, a forcing of truth home to the hearers' consideration, and a personal courage of conviction and presentation, are features which an audience will recognize with respect, or miss with dissatisfaction if not contempt.

To these must be added whatever of personal power the speaker may be endowed with.   By this power is meant that indefinable quality which interests, attracts, fas- Personal power. cinates, and commands.   Many speakers have all other endowments but this one.   A few have it in moderate measure, and fewer still have it in such marvellous degree that it covers many deficiencies, and makes the possessors for the time as princes among their fellow-men. It has various names, of which " personal magnetism " is the commonest.   But whatever it be called, there is no mistaking its presence, and no substitution for its absence.   To analyze it is as impossible as to tabulate the sweet influences of Pleiades, to weigh the sunshine, or to measure the storm. It is an ultimate fact, an inheritance, a gift. He who possesses a good voice has one of the priceless gifts; a good presence is another; reasoning powers, imagination, readiness of speech, others still; but like the gift of charity among the virtues is this personal power, the very spirit and soul of eloquence. Sympathy is no doubt its chief constituent: for unsympathetic speakers are known to have little of this magnetic power. It is sure to find expression in sympathetic tones which come from the heart rather than the head. The same sympathetic quality will get into thoughts and words, and find its response in kindred emotions, which in turn will react upon the speaker, and communicate themselves like contagion from rank to rank of hearers. Yet after the last analysis there is a residue of power which cannot be accounted for. It is as the mighty remnant which is the controlling influence holding the balance of power the world over,—the little salt in the ocean that prevents corruption, the little breeze that prevents stagnation, the few righteous men who save the city. Such a gift it is that saves some speakers from utter failure, or again gives to pre-eminent talents their crowning perfection. It is the secret of much eloquence which lives only in tradition, because its power can never be discovered in the record itself of the oratorical triumphs. Rare as the blooming of the aloe, it is known by the following it draws, and the admiring crowd around it. No age has failed to recognize it when it has appeared, nor to pay it the same homage from the beginning until now. Other means of enlightening, instructing, and moving the masses have come into competition and are doing their work well and faithfully, but this one is not yet supplanted. Nothing has hitherto been discovered to take the place of the personal power which the eye, the tongue, and the living, speaking presence have over men, to impel them to immediate action, or to inspire them with noble sentiments. Therefore, those who have this gift should cherish it as if it were an occult quality and a magician's rod. Those who have it only in a small degree may increase it by following its evident pointings. By being sympathetic, interested in the affairs which interest others, earnest, open minded, and generous hearted, voicing the better thoughts of men as they themselves would utter them if they could,—these are the invisible constituents of a power which is behind all supreme eloquence.

Yet great as this gift is, it must be accompanied by what the ancients called the ethical The ethical quality. quality, of which they made the greatest account as an element of power with hearers.   For they recognized the instinctive sympathy which an assembly has with what is right.   It may be swayed for a short time to the wrong side of a question by artful appeal to its ignorance, prejudice, or passion, but when the right and the wrong are fairly presented the popular conscience springs back to the line of truth and equity, and the sober thought and the impulse of its better sentiment spontaneously applaud the nobler utterance.   Therefore in the end the ruling majority demand right thinking and true speaking from the orator in whom they are to put their trust for counsel in times of perplexity

and doubt.   They will accept his guidance because he represents what is honorable and just.
To ally himself with this fundamental equity,
or better still to be true to his own inborn
sense of it, is the speaker's citadel of power,
the stronghold of his best reserves.   From this
rock he cannot be permanently driven by in-
genious arts of adversaries.   Around it the
forces that control opinion will rally in critical
emergencies.   On it the wise speaker will stand
because it is greater than his own conviction,
stronger than his words, mightier than his personality.   These may be mutable, fallible,
ephemeral.   But fundamental truth and justice
are unchangeable, and in their hold upon men
are practically constant.   To these standards
they are naturally loyal, and they will involun-
tarily respond to the man who is true to what
is best in himself and in them.   Herein lies
the source of his greatest power.

PART III.

FORMS OF OCCASIONAL ADDRESS.

I.

THE EULOGY.

IN enumerating the methods of discussion appropriate to demonstrative oratory in a former chapter, special mention was made of the descriptive and representative modes of portraying character. Examples were also cited of memorial and commemorative addresses in which this method prevails. Still other and more famous memorials of illustrious lives have adorned the record of demonstrative oratory from the earliest times. For next to the military harangue, before or after a battle, which characterized the early eloquence of nations, especially of the Greeks from the time of Pisistratus to the close of the Persian war, it is probable that the panegyric of the dead is the primeval form of the occasional address.

A primeval form of address.

Its germ is seen in such a remote fragment as David's lament for the first king of Israel

Hebrew, Greek, and Roman panegyric.

and his son, slain together on the mountains of Gilboa; and again in such an apostrophe as that of Demosthenes to the heroes of Marathon and Platea. Its later and fuller development is symbolized by compositions like the funeral oration of Hyperides over Leosthenes and his comrades who fell in the Lamian war; or that of Plato and Pericles over those who fell in the first battles of the Peloponesian war, if Thucydides version of them be correct, as given in the second chapter of his history, and in Plato's *Menexenus*. Indeed, these two examples of epidictic oratory are pre-eminent among the performances of Hellenic speakers. The colossal majesty of treatment which the subject receives at the hands of Pericles is characterized by a breadth of view and calmness of judgment which forbids idle intrusiveness, and the impertinence of captious criticism. It towers above the distractions of this middle earth in the regions of a supernal atmosphere, making the reader feel that the orator belonged to an age when it was believed that gods and men held converse together. More human, but more powerful, is the emotional eulogium of the impassioned Plato, who allied his countrymen to their native soil—the nourishing mother of heroes, making rival contestants brothers in their concord—and devotion to the land which bore and reared them, outside of which the world was barbarian, but within was to be a united family of one Hellenic purpose and destiny. To such an order of composition must also be referred the panegyrical efforts at a contest instituted by Artemisia in honor of Mausolus, her husband, at which many of Isocrates's pupils contested for the prize which Theopompus won. Also Gorgias' '' Epitaphian Oration,'' a fragment of which constitutes all his work now extant, is another example of commemorative eulogium. The so-called '' Funeral Oration '' of Demosthenes, by whomsoever composed, serves for a type of the panegyric, while the better example by Lysias and, surpassing all, the exalted and eulogistic speeches of Thucydides are a revelation to our time, of the height and depth to which Hellenic speakers carried this branch of demonstrative eloquence. Into this tribute of honor to the worthy dead they wove broad bands of patriotism, ancestral pride, national honor, and renewed devotion to ruling ideas, meantime enriching literature by undying models of commemorative eloquence.

In a later and Latin age a conspicuous example of this kind of oratory is found in a panegyric addressed to the Emperor Trajan by Pliny the younger. His letter to the emperor concerning the imperial policy toward Christians is more familiar than this " laudation " of royalty to its face, in return for the appointment of the orator to the governorship of Bythinia. It was a time when kings expected to be praised, and when it was safer to overdo the matter than to fall short. Yet in this case there was evidently good sense on both sides, and the minimum of flattery is bestowed. Felicitous passages abound, and the elegance which was valued in a decadent age is not wanting,—an age whose decline Pliny's better taste and unquestioned authority did much to retard. Looked upon,

Panegyrists of imperialism.

however, from present levels of self-respecting independence, it is easy to pronounce a less charitable sentence, and say with a modern critic, that this effusion is " a piece of courtly flattery, for the fulsomeness of which the only defence is the cringing and fawning manners of the time." But once more it should be remembered, that the best canons of historical criticism make allowance for a man's environment, whatever may be the proper judgment of absolute right and wrong. It was an age when it was customary to address the emperor as " Your Eternity." Considering that the length of the reigns of Trajan's five predecessors averaged less than ten years each, this panegyric of Pliny's was pitched below the customary tone of court adulation. Moreover, the tribute to Trajan's virtue became proverbially just two and a half centuries after his death.

Besides the above example there are eulogies on the Roman emperors in the third and fourth centuries. Their chief value is in the light they throw on the literary character of the times rather than in their oratorical excellence:

14

for it was a period of poor taste and subservi-ence to despotism and false ideals.   The authors of any note are Claudius Mamertinus, Eumenius, Nazarius, and Latinus Pacatus. Less extravagant, and perhaps even better de-served than most of these, is Ambrose's eulogy upon Gratian and Valentinian, A.D. 392, and incidentally upon the decadent glory of an im-perialism which ended with Theodosius three years later, in so far as the maintenance of the full dignity of the Roman name is concerned. Other examples of commemorative discourse might be cited, and more were delivered than were recorded in ages when oratory was strongly demonstrative, and when the subjects of it were the mighty dead.

Feudalism was an atmosphere in which the growth of panegyric was rank.   The king, the

pope, and the kaiser, the crusader, the baron, and the liege lord, the hermit, the abbot, and the bishop, called forth the loyal tribute of preachers who, for the oc-casion, were the spokesmen of the people and the proclaimers of their allegiance and devo-tion.   It is, however, after the revival of learning, and in the remarkable age of culture which was coeval with the reign of Louis Fourteenth, that this form of demonstrative eloquence appears as the flower and fruit of antecedent literary achievement. The funeral orations of Flechier, " the Isocrates of France," are examples whose first oratorical triumph was a discourse on the death of the Duchess of Montausier, followed by the oration upon Turenne. These performances placed him on a level with the illustrious trio who made the age famous for commemorative eloquence, Bossuet, Bourdaloue, and Massillon. Other examples of his power were the orations upon Lamoignon, Queen Maria Theresa, and the Chancellor, Le Tellier, to which may be added the three volumes of panegyrics of the saints. Three contemporaries of Flechier, mentioned above, were distinguished for their *oraisons funebres*, Massillon in particular, whose eulogy at the obsequies of Louis le Grand became famous for the simplicity of its opening sentence: " *Dieu seul est grand, mes amis.*" Other famous panegyrics of his were the funeral discourses at the death of the Prince of

Conti, 1709, of the Dauphin, the following year, and of the Duchess of Orleans in 1723.

The memorial discourse reached its highest development as literature in the celebrated *eloges* of the French Academy.   By virtue of his office it falls to the permanent secretary to pronounce a eulogy after the death of one of the members of any of the colleges which constitute, after many vicissitudes, the present National Institute of France. In the course of its diversified career notable men have been eulogized by others equally famous, and since the first Academy was founded, in 1635, there has been time to amass a literature of the eulogy formidable in its proportions.   Thirty-three years of Condorcet's service alone fill two volumes; Fontenelle contributes two more, containing the memorial addresses for forty-two years of his distinguished secretaryship as an eminent savant. Among the illustrious subjects which he commemorated were Malebranche, Leibnitz, Newton, Boerhave, Perrault, treating them with a justice which attributed no qualities not possessed, and exaggerated none that were.   He

was content to exhibit the great points in
every character, and let the small ones alone.
Equally illustrious are the thirty names embalmed by Louis, and others still by Thomas
and by D'Alembert, the last of whom delivered
orations upon the lives and characters of Massillon, Boileau, St. Pierre, Bossuet, Cousin,
Colbert, Montesquieu, and Saint Cyr. Vicq-
d'Azyr recalls the learning, the labors, and
the virtues of Duhamel, Bergman, Vergennes,
Cuvier, Pariset, Mignet, Dubois, and Flourens.
In all these tributes, differing with different
eulogists and diverse characters, there will not
fail to be found the Gallic sense of fitness and
the adaptation of the discourse to its subject.
The closing summaries in some of them are
graphic delineations, answering to Fenelon's
definition of the eulogy as " vivifying the arts
and exciting emulation," while they also meet
Voltaire's designation of it as a " perfume
reserved for embalming the dead." In this
place may be cited one or two other estimates
of what the eulogy should be, notably Mme.
de Glenlis's, who said that the indirect praise
is the only one that can make an impression,

having all the force of indirect testimony as
evidence.   Here also it may be well to note
the distinctions which a discriminating people
like the French make between the funeral
discourse, "religious in character," and the
eulogy, "not so of necessity, but simple in
style" while the panegyric is "pompous with
the trappings of a gorgeous rhetoric."

Sometimes the mania for eulogizing carried
panegyrists almost as far as a similar enthusiasm drove later Romans when they praised
"dust and smoke" in Fronto's day; or as
when Syenesius, a disciple of Hypatia, extolled
poverty in the fifth century, and Favorinus
glorified deformity; or as when a thousand
years after Erasmus wrote a volume in praise
of folly.   Of course there is no reason why
things may not be eulogized as well as men,
especially since, as in the case of
abstract virtues, they present no
detracting qualifications, and are
therefore easy and safe to praise.   On the
other hand, the human character, which is the
result of native endowments and inheritances
placed in a world of good and evil influences,

becomes a more legitimate subject of praise if it pass through these creditably and honorably. For such attainment and achievement, according to its degree in each instance, there may be words of commendation in justice to the departed, and for an inspiration to the living. According to such a general sentiment it is, therefore, probable that the eulogy in some of its forms—commemorative address, memorial sermon, funeral oration, or panegyric—will always be recognized as an appropriate tribute to be paid to exceptional worth. Whoever may be called upon to perform such an office will find an abundance of suggestion in directions that have been indicated, but by no means exhausted, in one of the most interesting phases of demonstrative speech.

In regard to the eulogy in Great Britain it must be said that while it has had a fair representation in English literature, especially in its ecclesiastical portions, British eulogy. the nation has provided other memorials for its illustrious departed. There has always been a reverent recognition of ancestral virtues, military, civil, and domestic, but it has likewise been tempered with modesty, sound judgment, and just criticism.   Therefore eminent examples of this form of eloquence are comparatively infrequent in English literature.   A poem, a biographical sketch, or a historical digression commemorating exceptional worth, are oftener found as mementos of departed greatness.   Tennyson's " In Memoriam " Macaulay's " Essay on Milton ," Green's chapters on Edward the Third, or Wolsey, or Thomas Cromwell, are examples of Englishmen's tributes to their illustrious countrymen.   Or in deliberative capacity, having offered brief and discriminating testimony to the worth of the dead, they turn to discuss matters relating to the commonweal, and leave memorials to be the care of relatives, or place them in the keeping of Westminster Abbey.   Burke has a brief characterization of Sir Joshua Reynolds, ending with a " Hail and Farewell "; Grattan sums up the abilities and talents of Lord Chatham in a few weighty paragraphs; Sir James Mackintosh performs the same service for the memory of Charles James Fox and for George Canning.   Of the last he said:

" He was a man of fine and brilliant genius, of warm affections, of a high and generous spirit—a statesman who, at home, converted most of his opponents into warm supporters ; who, abroad, was the sole hope and trust of all who sought an orderly and legal liberty, and who was cut off in the midst of vigorous and splendid measures, which, if executed by himself or with his own spirit, promised to place his name in the first class of rulers, among the founders of lasting peace and the guardians of human improvement."

Such is a moderate and fair encomium upon a distinguished parliamentary orator by one of his peers. It may stand as a type of the general tenor of British eulogy. With that nation, however, this moderation is more effective than the extravagant laudation which the orators of southern Europe and the East were accustomed to bestow upon their heroes, saints, and kings. In homiletic and forensic literature can be found much commemorative speech that has of necessity a local value. Of greater interest to the Anglo-Saxon race are the eulogistic creations of the English drama, whose exaltation of heroes is in the best spirit and the highest form of brief encomiastic speech.

When, however, English literature is transplanted to American soil it begins to take on new characteristics. A stimulating climate, a large freedom, and a generous hospitality toward all climes and ages give it at length a cosmopolitan receptivity and a wide adaptation.

Eulogy in America.   It is not afraid to follow French taste in letters, nor Greek, nor Roman, nor what of Italian or Spanish or German is worth absorbing and recreating.   Therefore so important an element as the eulogistic could not escape appropriation by a people which felt itself to be the inheritor of treasures that had been accumulating in all lands for centuries. There was, accordingly, in the early oratory of our country an almost boyish frequency of reference to classical antiquity.   But there was also a familiar acquaintance with its literature and laws which surpassed that of recent generations of educated men, who have so many things to learn that they cannot acquire much knowledge of any one thing.   Among the literary acquisitions of the fathers was some idea of the proper nature and limits of the eulogy.

It began with the beginnings of our own literature, in a time when all compositions were **Clerical memorials.**   almost endless in their continuance and fearful in their solemn tediousness.   Nevertheless they met the demand of a

much-enduring and patient-listening people; as
is evident from the account that when a
preacher, being ill, shortened his discourse to
two and a half hours, one of the brethren
apologized by saying, "We have a strong
weakness here in New England that when we
are speaking we know not how to conclude.
We make many ends before we end." But it
should be added that the Sunday sermon was
the chief entertainment of all the week in
Plymouth Colony and Massachusetts Bay.
Accordingly, when a man like John Cotton
became a subject of panegyric, the performance
was co-extensive with the industry of a scholar
who could study twelve consecutive hours each
day, and " sweeten his mouth with a piece of
John Calvin before he went to sleep." Upon
the admirable accomplishments and acquirements of such a " universal scholar and walk-
ing library," it is marvellous that his grandson,
Cotton Mather, of Magnalian prolixity, could
ever have made an end of his laudation. Judging by his customary " longitude in speech,"
as Nathaniel Ward terms it, he must have
occupied all the hours " from morn till noon,

from noon to dewy eve '' in an exposition of his ancestor's orthodoxy and his unparalleled '' gift of continuance.'' For a typical and clerical eulogy of the time the reader is commended to '' The Departure and Character of Elijah Considered and Improved—after the decease of the learned and Very Reverend Cotton Mather, D.D. and F.R.S., and Minister of the North Church in Boston. By Samuel Mather, M.A., Boston, 1726.'' Of such memorial discourses on the ministers of New England there are twenty octavo volumes extant, and five more on the ministers of Boston alone. In them may be traced the slow deliverance of American thought and expression from the painful cramps of seventeenth-century Puritanism; but still more evident is its lingering tenacity to ways that were both strait and angular. Now and then some bolder spirit struggles for elbow-room, as when in '' A Plain Memorative Account of Mr. Thomas Symmes '' one happens upon a note of slow progression as follows: '' He thought it was high time that our Common Custom of Reading the line in Singing should be laid aside, because of its very much interrupting the Melody and sometimes the Sense, and because the Reason of it now ceases, there being plenty of Psalm Books.'' But this is a digression from the customary and monotonous '' exercising '' upon the public and private ministrations and the circumspect virtues of several generations of religious teachers.

Among the four hundred and forty-three commemorative discourses, preserved in the Metcalf collection in the library of Brown University, one name or the other of the following pairs stands forth from a great company of forgotten worthies as not yet entirely lost in a fast gathering oblivion. Increase Mather is borne up by the family name, while Michael Wigglesworth, his subject, will have an immortality of his own by reason of his priority as an American versifier, established during a twenty-years' retirement for his health in the West Indies. Amid tropical scenes his stern spirit was melted into poetic mood, and the long-restrained muse of Massachusetts Bay burst forth into the ravishing strains of a poem called '' The Day of Doom,'' once the most popular verse in

New England. The most cheerful passage in it is that in which unbaptized infants are accorded " the easiest room in hell." In later days, Jonathan Edwards, whose theology was more fiery than his spirit, memorialized the saintly Branierd ; Channing discoursed on Worcester, Ware on Prentiss, Stiles on Whittlesey, Dwight on Goodrich, Onderdonk on White, Jarvis on Seabury, Wainwright on Duffie, Hobart on Moore, Manning on Estlin, Tyng on Milnor, Sears on Allen, Garnet on Peabody, Storrs on Park, Doane on Winslow, Frothingham on Gay, Park on Stuart, Bacon on Dutton, Seabury on White, Coxe on Seabury, Gano on Snow, Eastburn on Bristol, and Woodbridge on Williston. There are others among the four hundred and forty pairs remaining equally memorable, but " time would fail me to tell of the Gideons and Baraks and Samsons, of the Jephthahs, the Davids, the Samuels, and the prophets " in the long succession of New England worthies. Besides these there were eighty-eight Boston ministers who have five octavo volumes of commemoration all to themselves. Some have more than one discourse in their praise: Griswold three, Crosswell four, and Channing no less than eleven. Eighty-three wives of ministers are similarly honored, as they ought to have been, not only for sharing their husbands' trials, but also for the added trial of clerical husbands, themselves sorely tried by parochial infelicities. Mather Byles, of loyalist and literary fame, friend of Pope and Swift, heads the list with a funeral discourse on Anna his wife, taking a text from the Epistle to the Philippians, and a motto from Boëthius's *Consolations of Philosophy*. Other worthy women are commemorated to the number of one hundred and forty-six in this epitaphian collection. Twenty-five volumes are filled with the memorials of the lesser lights of New England, six hundred and forty-five in all, classed " Miscellaneous."

Not in this class by any means are the eulogies upon colonial magistrates, who ranked next to the ministers on one side or the other of them, both offices being sometimes merged in one personage. How important figures they were in early colonial days, and even in later, may be

Eulogies upon magistrates.

understood by reading Rev. William Cooper's discourse on William Tailer, " Lieutenant Governor of the Province of Massachusetts Bay in New England "—so his title ran in 1731; or Mr. Appleton's on " Lieutenant Governor Spencer Phipps, and Commander-in-chief of his Majesty's forces," 1757; or Thomas Thacher's on Governor Bowdoin; or Peter Thacher's on Governor John Hancock, or on Samuel Adams; or Abiel Holmes's (Oliver Wendell's father) on Governor Sumner (Charles's grandfather), 1799; or President Dwight's on Governor Trumbull, 1809. The tone of them all is symbolized by the words of Buckminster on Governor Sullivan:

" When I look back upon the successive generations of men and see how painfully they have been climbing to the heights of temporal grandeur, and observe the little brief authority, the panting ambition, the pitiable pride, the wreaths withered as soon as plucked, the grave opening under the very chair of supreme authority, I am ready to cry, God have mercy on the great, and forgive the pride of shortlived man when the naked spirit shall stand trembling in thy presence, and it is no longer remembered whether it expired on a scaffold or on a throne ! "

Of course there was due praise for what was worthy, but this sentiment underlay all else, as became men who feared God more than they feared the king. For the king they had loyalty so long as he was reasonable, and when he died he did not lack respectful mention. Accordingly, there were four moderate panegyrics on George the Second; three also on Queen Caroline, four on Frederick, Prince of Wales, and two on Princess Charlotte. Encomiums on the succeeding Georges would naturally be confined to loyalists after 1776, and the tributes of the majority be transferred to Washington and his successors. The first President was eulogized throughout the new nation in at least 129 sermons which were deemed worthy of publication, while the almost simultaneous death of Adams and Jefferson called out a multitude of addresses upon one or both, and the demise of President William Henry Harrison so soon after his inauguration elicited another flood of addresses, two volumes of which have been collected and preserved. Subsequent to the death of all the above dignitaries and of others, there have been estimates at different times of their lives and characters, one of the most celebrated being Edward Everett's famous oration upon Washington.

15

The foregoing outline of eulogistic literature might be considered as a qualification upon the character of demonstrative oratory if it were not remembered that, in any age, it equalled and sometimes surpassed other literary ventures. Compared with early attempts at historical, biographical, and especially poetical composition, it will not suffer. Polemical theology and controversy alone ranked with it in ability, while falling far behind it in more attractive elements of composition. And as the generations went by, commemorative speech improved with advancing literary taste, until in the last fifty years some of the best examples in the history of occasional oratory appear. Everett's oration upon Washington has been mentioned as the final term in an ascending series, an achievement which has not been since surpassed. There is abundant reason for calling it the perfect fruit of eulogistic speech, which had been ripening for two hundred years.

A brief examination of its origin and character will show why it holds this supreme place in our eulogistic literature. First, the writer himself had made demonstrative oratory the principal purpose of his literary career. Similar achievements had been accomplished by him with unusual credit, but this was his greatest success. Fitted by *Everett's eulogy upon Washington.* familiarity with the best of classic eloquence, himself possessing the spirit of its masters, endowed with its graces and imbued with patriotic zeal for the unity of the nation, whose history he knew by heart, and whose founders had but just passed from view, as historical eras are computed, Edward Everett was the man of all men to depict the character and virtues of Washington. Besides, the subject of his eulogy belonged to the entire community of States, and to all their inhabitants—a person of whose praises no section could tire. Add to this the object of the speaker—the purchase of Mount Vernon, to which the proceeds of this address, delivered without charge, and many times repeated North and South and West, contributed over fifty-three thousand dollars—ten thousand more being added by the earnings of the author's pen. The man, the subject, the object, and one hundred and fifty occasions conspired to give this production a prominence which no other eulogy has had in all the course of time.   Therefore it is eminently proper to look for a moment at its structure as a work of art.

The occasion.—Often the anniversary of Washington's birthday precluded the need of any extended insistence upon the importance of his theme, and accordingly three lines suffice for the announcement of his subject.

Analysis of the oration.

The introduction is proportionably brief in its allusion to the recommendation of Congress (in 1799), " that the people of the United States testify their grief for the death of General George Washington, by suitable eulogies, orations, and discourses." This furnishes an opportunity to mention the illustrious orators who have preceded him, Fisher Ames, Webster, and Winthrop, whose performances had taken an abiding place in the literature of the country, leaving little to be discussed anew. Therefore he craves permission to approach a familiar subject in a different direction. Thus he incidentally arouses a fresh interest in a well-worn topic, as has been shown above.

A *statement* follows of what he proposes to do,—" to offer some views of the relation of Washington, not merely to the United States, but to the age in which he lived, and then to point out the true nature and foundation and distinctive character of his greatness. " Grant me, my friends, your candor, your indulgence, and your sympathy."

The narration of Washington's early career in border hostilities, the approbation he received in Virginia and Massachusetts, his waiting in watchful retirement at Mount Vernon for his high commission as leader of the colonial forces is graphic in an assured certainty which marks the master:

" Years pass by ; the august plan of Providence ripens ; the beloved and revered chieftain, aided by his patriotic associates, carries the bleeding country through another seven years' war,—hard apprenticeship of freedom, . . . thirteen independent State governments succeed to as many Colonies,—peace crowns the work. . . . America takes her place in the family of nations."

With a tribute to his compatriots, among whom, however, he was as " fixed and constant as the Northern Star," he passes directly to the first year of his administration as Presi-

dent of the new Union under the Constitution,
at the age of fifty-seven and in the year 1789.

The *character portrait* which he is going to
paint has a background which the speaker de-
picts with strong and free hand—the age in
which he lived,

" a period," he remarks, "which in many respects stands first
in the annals of our race for great names, great events, great
reforms, and the general progress of intelligence, the age of
wonders in the history of mankind."   ;

With equal rapidity and precision the orator
then proceeds to fill in the sketch by grouping
the mighty men of Europe and the East, and
enumerating events in the manner of a philosophic historian from cause to effect, from the
Sclavonic movements in the steppes of North-
western Asia and the conquest of Hindoostan,
to the English victory on the heights of Que-
bec, and the American triumph at Yorktown ;
from Peter the Great and Catherine the Second,
from Clive and Wolfe to him who was greater
than all, the brightest ornament of an age
that therefore should be called the Age of
Washington.

By comparison he then proceeds to give the
measure and stature of the man, choosing three

standards of estimation which the world has regarded as the greatest of that time—Peter the
Great, Frederick the Second, and Napoleon.
The greatness of each he shows was qualified
by notorious defects, and lacked the symmetry
which signalizes the character of Washington.

Emphasis is laid upon this harmonious development of all virtues by asserting that it was
original, not borrowed, having no illustrious
example of this kind of excellence to follow in
a crude age and in a land without great traditions and institutions and characters. " Like
Columbus, Washington and his compatriots
were compelled to sound their way along un-
visited coasts of republican government and
constitutional liberty." He had to be a leader
with no pioneer breaking the way before him,—
without precedent or beacon in the ancient or
modern world to guide him. " I see many who
deserved well of their country, . . . but I
behold in the long line no other Washington,
solitary in his eminence among the great and
good."

A definition follows of what this eminence
consisted in, or rather the admission of inability

to describe that impalpable essence and latent power which marks supreme character.   Other men have confessed to the same inability '' to paint the sunbeam with a brushful of flake white.''   He falls back on the tradition of '' a serene dignity which both charmed and awed the boldest who approached him.''

An answer is here interposed to the qualifying and faint praise of those foreign critics who deny the crown of genius to Washington, while they accord him eminent rank as a '' chieftain, magistrate, and patriot.''   If he could conduct the nation through the war of the Revolution, and the period of no government which followed it, and through his two administrations set an example for all future presidents to follow; if he could do this without genius, then its possession would have been of little consequence.   But so far from being a defect, the excellence of his character consists in the exclusion of inordinately developed traits, which usually constitute genius, and destroy the symmetry of a well-rounded character in its perfection of proportion and balance.   This ideal, to be sure, is one of which the populace has little apprehension, while for prudence, justice, modesty, and good sense, it has little admiration and no great liking. This criticism is then made with true Parthian skill to contribute to the eulogist's vindication and laudation of his subject in the words: " Instead, therefore, of being a mark of inferiority, this sublime adjustment of powers and virtues in the character of Washington is in reality its glory."

A comparison with four military geniuses—Alexander, the Duke of Marlborough, and Napoleon Bonaparte—strengthens and illustrates the position he has taken on the supremacy of a well-balanced character over one-sided though dazzling brilliancy. Folly, avarice, and rashness were successively the ruin of three men of genius, and ambitious usurpation the death of Julius Cæsar, the fourth. Fontanes, whom Napoleon selected to eulogize Washington in France, called him truly " the pure, the just, the humane, the unambitious." Four words could not have been better chosen, though unconsciously, to show that Washington was strong where the others were despicably weak or unwise.

The conclusion begins with a continuance of testimony to his greatness, of which Hamilton said, that " the voice of praise would in vain endeavor to exalt a name unrivalled in the lists of true glory "; and Fox, voicing English sentiment, said, " A character of virtues so happily tempered by one another, and so wholly unalloyed with any vices, is hardly to be found on the pages of history." Therefore it belongs to Americans to show respect for Washington by obedience to his words in the Farewell Address exhorting them to preserve the Union in its integrity—the hope of the Republic.

An appeal follows which recalls the adjuration of Demosthenes, remembering Marathon, beginning: " No, by the glorious nineteenth of April, 1775; by the precious blood of Bunker Hill, of Princeton, of Saratoga, of King's Mountain, of Yorktown; by the undying spirit of '76; by the sacred dust enshrined at Mount Vernon; by the dear immortal memory of Washington, that shame and sorrow shall never be." And with a strain of prophecy, " that ever, as the twenty-second of

February returns, the memory of the greatest man of a great age shall be renewed and cherished in all the land," the eulogy, which is worthy of its theme, comes to an end.

To recapitulate its divisions: they are,—Introduction, Statement, Narration, Portraiture, Comparison, Main Proposition, Definition, Refutation by Contrast, Conclusion. To apprehend how much hangs upon these points, or even upon the preceding outline, the whole oration should be read. It will be seen that while there have been as eloquent productions, even upon less distinguished subjects, none have surpassed this one in adaptation to the character eulogized and in the classic severity and harmonious proportion of treatment. It will always stand as another monument to Washington, as worthy a memorial as is the shaft which perpetuates his memory in the city that bears his name.

There are passages of rare beauty in this eulogy which it would be pleasant to note; but such observation must be deferred until minuter features of commemorative discourse are considered.

The Eulogy as a form of demonstrative oratory might be dropped here, were it not that a few other examples would be missed by anyone expecting a fair enumeration of the best work that has been done in this direction. Everett himself, under the modest title of " Remarks," gave characterizations of Prescott the historian, of Henry Hallam, of Alexander von Humboldt, of Rufus Choate, of Washington Irving, of Nathan Appleton, Professor Felton, Nathan Hale, Josiah Quincy, and President Lincoln, and others.   More elaborate efforts were pronounced in memory of Thomas Dowse, showing what he could do with a humble subject; of Daniel Webster, a great one; and in the " Vindication of American Institutions," a broad one; and, at the Consecration of the National Cemetery at Gettysburg,—an oration in which the heroic memories of Marathon are revived once more, and the spirit of Hellenic eloquence, always latent in this orator, finds an inviting opportunity for utterance.

Amongst the judicial and deliberative speeches of Daniel Webster his commemorative addresses on Washington, and on Adams and Jefferson, show what he could do in the direction of demonstrative elo- quence. Robert C. Winthrop, an Other eulogists. occasional orator, and during his active life a speaker on almost every public occasion, adds to his numerous short addresses longer memorials of the life of James Bowdoin, and of Barnas Sears, and a eulogy on George Peabody; while his oration at the laying of the corner-stone of the national monument to Washington in 1848, and another on its completion in 1885, partake of the nature of commemorative discourse. His frequent brief addresses in memory of one and another celebrated man of his time as they passed away, are models of their kind in a difficult branch of public speech. In the midst of forensic labors, such as fall to the fortune of few eminent lawyers, Rufus Choate made room for eulogies of rare beauty and truth upon President William Henry Harrison in Faneuil Hall in 1841, and on Daniel Webster before the faculty and students of Dartmouth College in 1853.

In addition to those already enumerated

elsewhere may be mentioned among note-worthy eulogies, memorial and commemora-tive addresses that of George Bancroft upon the life and character of Abraham Lincoln, de-livered before both Houses of Congress on the 12th of February, 1866; the eulogy of William M. Evarts upon William H. Seward; of James G. Blaine upon James A. Garfield; Senator Lamar's tribute to Charles Sumner; William C. Bryant's addresses on Cooper, Halleck, and Irving ; Emerson's memorial of Thoreau; Robert C. Winthrop's of George Peabody; Oliver Wendell Holmes's of Motley and Emerson; George William Curtis's eulogies upon Sumner, Phillips, Bryant, and Lowell; Parke Godwin's on Curtis, Edwin Booth, Kossuth, Audubon, and Bryant; and others by other distinguished men, often in composi-tions of equal excellence, until the last orator who maintained the high place of the eulogy became silent. This was George William Curtis, whose eulogies on Charles Sumner, James A. Garfield, Wendell Phillips, William C. Bryant, and James Russell Lowell are, taken together, unsurpassed by any similar number in the entire literature of eulogistic speech.

Judging, then, by recent example it is evident, that its day has not passed. Compared with judicial and deliberative ora- _{Permanence of the eulogy.} tory, as they are found in the courts and the legislative assemblies of the land, the quality of demonstrative speech in its commemorative phase will hold its own. Nor is there immediate likelihood that the custom of honoring the praiseworthy, and commemorating good in human lives, will be discontinued. In particular, the acts and character of memorable and distinguished persons will be a subject of demonstrative discourse. If, as is usually the case when such addresses are delivered, the life here has ended, such discourse will assume naturally the tone of eulogy. It is the good in men's lives that should live after them, and it becomes the office of the memorial address to drop the evil, the imperfections, the venial faults, and to perpetuate the virtues, the noble aspirations, and the higher ideals toward which endeavor was made in spite of weights which dragged, and burdens which bowed down the spirit. Such eulogy has often been condemned as partiality and one-sided unreality; but it may be questioned if it is not in harmony with that law which tends to slough off the old and put on the new, to drop the crude and assume the ripening state, to leave that which is temporal and mortal for the immortal and spiritual. To drag up to public gaze the imperfect and the incomplete side of a person's life is contrary to this law. The only apology for this sort of candor is in cases where the bad preponderates, and is to be shown up for admonition. But, the subject being a worthy one, it is only just that its fair side be presented, as one would wish his friend's portrait painted, not in a moment of perplexity, trouble, or passion, but in an hour of serenity, perhaps of gladness or bright anticipation.

Assuming that so much will be granted for the tone of discourse, it may be asked if any directions can be gathered from the *Principles of its construction.* literature of eulogistic speech for the guidance of those who may be called to perform this kindly office for one who is worthy of it. The first suggestion has been made already concerning fidelity of portraiture. It should be faithful indeed, but faithful to the best phases of character rather than the worst, to the ideal or better thought and sober intention and considerate action.

The next precept that may be gathered from the words of great panegyrists is, that the main and strong features of character are to be emphasized, rather than insignificant traits. Common sense dictates such a treatment, but its suggestions are not always followed. Then, too, the lesser traits are sometimes purposely magnified, in order to destroy the due balance and proportion of all, which is in effect a falsification, as far as it goes. It cannot be called idealization, which is making the best of the man as he was in the true relation and perspective of all his traits. To destroy that relation and distort the perspective is worse than nothing for him who is commemorated. The Chinese landscape painting, which puts insignificant and distant objects in the foreground, is neither ideal nor real art. It is simply a ridiculous distortion. There is, moreover, in every character a ruling purpose, ambition, or principle.   Around this as a centre of gravity every other motive revolves at a greater or less distance.   The entire life and character becomes the outgrowth of such a central fact.   The poise and equipoise of impulse and purpose gather about it, and in turn the ruling principle becomes the index of a life. Therefore it is to be sought and seized upon as a key to character.   In most men it is some form of ambition, according to their natural bent.   Where there is no sort of ambition there will be little to commemorate when life is ended.   And some ambitions are not worth commemorating at all.   The memorialist will accordingly ask in the beginning, What does this completed life stand for ?   What cardinal and ruling idea does it represent with more or less intensity and fulness ?   This central principle once determined, it becomes easier to range other prominent traits in their proper order, so many of them as it may be needful to dwell upon, and the rest it may be sufficient simply to enumerate.

It would not be fair to avoid the question which is always arising in regard to the treat-

ment of disagreeable features and characteristics. In full view of what has been said
already about the universal tendency
of nature to throw off the imperfect
and the bad, it may nevertheless be
admitted that some recognition of it, as an
element with which a conflict was waged, gives
to the eulogy a flavor of honesty and fairness
that otherwise might be lacking. Virtues are
also brought out into stronger relief by their
propinquity to defects and faults. The difficulty is always to keep the right relation
between the evil and the good. Here, as
everywhere, the taste of the eulogist will be the
test of his fitness for his task. That it is a
difficult task any one who undertakes it will
find before it is finished, unless it be a labor of
love, admiration, or devotion. But the compensations may be greater than the labor. In
any case, the examples of satisfactory achievement in this difficult and delicate sphere of
public address are so many and so instructive
that the well-informed man need not feel that
he must pursue an untrodden path. His main
inquiry will be only as to the direction he is to

take in the particular instance before him, what
way-marks he is to observe, what points he is
to linger over and lovingly portray, and what
ones he can pass lightly by.   And at the end
he will ask, Have I sketched truly and boldly
the strong features of a completed character, as
those who knew it best will recall it when the
future shall eliminate the petty and the imperfect, and leave only the best and the imperishable ?   For such is the sentiment of the living
who remember their dead.   The imperfections
and faults which annoyed and sometimes ex-
asperated, are forgotten as the oblivious years
move on, while what was best in life and character brightens in blessed remembrance—a reflection perhaps from the radiant cloud on some
mount of transfiguration in the world beyond.

II.

THE COMMEMORATIVE ADDRESS.

DEMONSTRATIVE oratory has for its proper subject-matter both persons and things. In this last general term may be included a wide range of themes not strictly professional in character. Events important or memorable, truths of present value and emphasis, princi- ples which may need stating, restating, or enforcing,—these all are appropriate topics of occasional discourse. Sometimes these two branches of demonstrative speech are unavoidably mingled, as when a person's life is shown to be the symbol of some virtue or general truth, or again where a far-reaching principle is illustrated by pertinent biographical example and incident. In this second class of discourse, however, there is less occasion to commingle the personal and the general in large proportions of each, and the separation between the two becomes distinct. Moreover, the treatment of subjects in the general or abstract form will of necessity differ somewhat from that of the concrete and personal embodiment of them. To unfold and illustrate this mode of discussion will be the object of the present chapter.

As in the case of the eulogy, the literature of this form of the occasional address is abundant; and the inductive method which teaches one how to proceed in constructive processes by examples of what has been done by others is as available in this section of the subject as in the other.

The beginnings of this literature also are remote. After the prowess and glory of the *Beginnings of commemorative literature.* chieftain had been extolled, came the celebration of the event in which he took so great a part. But, as the individual came to be of less and less account and the multitude of more and more, the event and the wide-prevailing movement, the principle of action, or the repetition of history made themselves the objects of thought and the subjects of speech.   Such transition from the person to the event is often apparent in primitive literatures, the Hebraic for example.   From discourse about the individual, his ancestor, or son, his own tribe, its leader, or champion, the address soon takes up laws, civil and ceremonial, the rewards of obeying them, and the penalty for breaking them; or, as has already been said, the speaker turns from the warrior to the war, from the king to his acts, his policy, his government, and in later times to their consequences as foretold in prophecy mingled with praise and blame, with assurances of perpetuity or with predictions of calamity, captivity, and destruction.   The same tendency is observable in " the bible of the nations," the Homeric literature, coincident with the Davidic period of our own Scriptures.   Achilles' wrath is for a time soon left, like himself, upon the shore, in his own hut, and by his own black ship, while the fortunes of the well-greaved Achæans occupy the poet's pen.   And on the other side of the Dardan plain it is not Paris nor even Helen, but the fate of the horse-taming Tro-

jans concerning whom those harangues are
made which, with Argive speeches, fill the
greater half of the *Iliad*. In succeeding oratory, as recorded by the historians who followed
the epic poets, there is a similar turning from
persons to events, from military chieftains to
their victories or defeats, and the consequences
that ensued; from rulers to statecraft, from
legislatures to legislation, from Xerxes and
Philip and Alexander to the many heroes of
Marathon, Platea, and Salamis first, and then
to the endangered liberties of Greece, the policy
of union against Persian invasion, and of resistance to Macedonian encroachment.

The same drift from the individual and personal concern and attention, to the general and
national, took place in Latin discourse so long
as liberty lasted, and until a despot drew all
speech back to himself in the form of open adulation or secret malediction. The movement
itself is in accord with that of all true advance
in the social and civil life of men and nations,
from the particular to the general, from the
importance of the personage to the greater importance of the community and the state. It

is also in harmony with the movement and growth of the human intellect from its observation of the single instance to the perception of the general law, and from the concrete example to the abstract principle.

In accordance with this general tendency it will be in order to observe with some care the literature of this class of demonstrative speech, as preparatory to the derivation from it of sundry principles and precepts which may guide one in the construction of an occasional oration or address upon a subject which is general rather than personal in character. The difference between such subjects will be seen the easier, if illustrated by the examples of Curtis's eulogy on Bancroft or Lowell, and the same speaker's oration upon " The American Doctrine of Liberty, or The Leadership of Educated Men."

In a historical view of this literature from the age where literary history begins to be continuous and definite, the oration, as distinguished from the eulogy, appears with increasing frequency. It *Historical survey of this literature.* may be not without interest to note, however,

that at the point of departure in Greek eloquence, it is mingled with the eulogy. If the
celebrated funeral oration which Thucydides
attributes to Pericles be taken as the first
example of a fairly reported speech in the
literature of Hellenic oratory, then it may be
conceded that the first example also of the occasional oration is to be found in this masterly
discourse.   For besides eulogizing the brave
men who were slain in the first year of the
Peloponesian war, the orator unfolds his conception of " an ideal civilization, and a fully
accomplished and established imperial city,"
which should be the Periclean Athens.   Here
then we have a transition resembling other
transitions in literature,—Theodectes', for instance, already mentioned.   It occurs in the
speech of an orator who discourses not only of
the heroic dead, but also of an ideal civilization, illustrated and enforced by the contrast
between Athens and Sparta.   The Athenian
system, he asserted, set an example to the
other Hellenic states in the way of national
power, and also in the development of the individual.   Frankness and liberality were traits

of its democracy; and public dignities were not dependent upon social grades, while every citizen was to concern himself about the laws. The amenities of life were to be cultivated, irksome discipline minimized without making men unequal to the demands of conflict or fearful of danger. Open-mindedness towards the stranger, publicity in discussion, promptness in legislation, courage in action, guided by reason in counsel, were all Athenian characteristics, substantiated by the fact that Athens proved always superior to her reputation when the trial came.

Not remotely related to the eulogy, then, is what, for the sake of distinction from it, may be called the Commemorative Address. The one is a memorial of a person, the other of an event. Both aim at perpetuating something which is worth saving from oblivion, and extending into the future what is too valuable to be restricted to the brief period when it was present among mankind. As between the two, the event is often of less duration than a lifetime; but as the issue of causes that have been long in operation, and as a result of●vast consequence to multitudes, the event may assume an importance out of all proportion to the time occupied in its actual occurrence.   Even so long and tedious and calamitous an event as either of the two great wars in our own country is short when compared with the entire life of any one of the principal men engaged in it; but the results of such wars are beyond computation in their enduring importance.   Therefore the commemoration of an event may well tax the best abilities of an orator.

The kind of event which is usually commemorated is one to which a people may refer with pride.   Not always with unmixed gladness; for sad memories to the individual are almost always inseparable from any great gain that accrues to the community or the nation, according to a well-known law of sacrifice.   But the defeat, the misfortune, and the disaster, seldom call for commemoration.   The labor of the speaker, accordingly, in this class of demonstrative speech is even pleasanter than in the eulogistic class.   No qualification or criticism is expected.

Interpretation and reminiscence.

Panegyric would be more excusable. The event is impersonal, and commendable; often a source of gratification and of honest, honorable pride. The speaker's business is to show why it is, and to derive from it legitimate lessons which shall strengthen, encourage, and inspire. Reminiscence is the chief burden and purpose of such discourse. By recalling the high achievement of those times and seasons when the people and their leaders have risen to the level of a great demand or a great opportunity, their successors are made familiar with attainments above the ordinary doings of everyday life, and are prepared for similar achievements when their opportunity also shall arrive. It is the oratory of the ideal founded upon the real; the eloquence of romance resting upon fact.

The earliest examples in the literature of such eloquence are full of reminiscence as an inspiring motive. " Remember the day when thou camest forth out of Egypt " is the burden of Moses' encouraging exhortation to Israel in the days of their despair and fear before their enemies;

Early examples : Hebrew.

and the prophets after him are continually re-
viving the memory of the nation's deliverance.
In all prophetic oratory there is a retrospective
element as well as a prospective, a constant
mindfulness of glorious events and of the
greater glory of prosperous ages in the history
of the nation. The leadership of Moses, and
Samuel, and David; the wisdom of Solomon,
and the splendor of the first temple linger in
the memory of Hebrew orators as inspiring
records of a nation's possibilities, so long as it
kept in the right way, and turned not aside
from truth and equity and righteousness.
This reminiscent tendency took on an expression stronger than words in the anniversary
feast-days such as the three great festivals of
the ancient Jewish people, or like that of
Purim, kept until the present day in memory
of the nation's deliverance from Haman's
malicious plot in the reign of Ahasuerus. But
it is more than probable that no such commemorative festival ever passed without the
commemorative discourse, explaining the
meaning of the feast to the young, and enforcing its lessons for the old. Israel had not

yet escaped from Pharaoh when by special command of its great law-giver such instruction was enjoined in connection with the feast of the Passover, as may be seen in the twelfth chapter of the book of Exodus: '' And it shall come to pass when your children say unto you, What mean ye by this service ? that ye shall say, It is the sacrifice of the Lord's passover, who passed over the houses of the children of Israel in Egypt when He smote the Egyptians and delivered our houses.'' To this day the event is explained to successive generations of Hebrews, as also the meaning of the greater Christian feast of Easter, in memory of a greater deliverance than that from Egyptian bondage, is set forth every year in all Christendom.

Among the nations outside the narrow strip of Palestine it is certain that a similar habit of commemoration prevailed. The multitude of memorial festivals *In other nations.* which grew up with mythological forms of religion or superstition attests the hold which reminiscence had upon the mind of antiquity. It was always turning toward a golden or heroic age, as is the bent of the human mind at all times.   Not to mention the festivals for the purpose of honoring or supplicating the gods, those for commemorating persons and events grew increasingly numerous as luxury and wealth increased.   This multiplicity is especially evident at Athens, because the record of it survives; but there is no reason to suppose that a similar abundance of such festivals did not prevail in the Egyptian or Assyrian empires.   The very general commemoration of whatever the names of Adonis or Thammuz represented is one of the earliest examples of the retrospective tendency; as are also the festivals of Bacchus, Diana, Aphrodite, Ceres, Apollo, and Jupiter, emblematical all of some power or phase of nature, which it is reasonable to suppose was not unexplained to the participants.   It was, however, at the most distinguished of the four grand and solemn games of the Greeks that the literature of commemoration would be most likely to be cultivated: for at Olympia the contests in poetry, history, and oratory could not fail to perpetuate the meaning and memory of the festival itself, whatever else they celebrated.

When Greek oratory began to be cultivated as a fine art it took on a practical character, growing out of the necessities of litigation and legislation. Therefore commemorative speech is not so common as judicial and deliberative, but now and then the memorial element appears in speeches, as might be expected among a people who dwell with fond pride upon a creditable antiquity. If, however, the entire class of epidictic oratory be considered, it will be found that it was a more powerful factor in the formation of a national literature than either the judicial or the deliberative. For its best work was written to be read, as well as to be spoken, and its composers labored as long and carefully over an oration as the poets over a drama. Isocrates was employed ten years on his famous *Panegyric*, whose central thought is Hellenic unity against the barbarian, radiating into a widening circle of subordinate propositions. The followers of Isocrates also did much to establish a prose literature which was more to the popular taste than the judicial or deliberative styles of oratory. Its influence passed even into the composition of historical works. Other orations of Isocrates which may be classed as demonstrative are the *Areopagiticus*, containing the contrast between the former social life and the later; also "The Encomium of Helen," with its praise of beauty in the abstract. Lysias also delivered epidictic speeches before the great Panhellenic assembly at the Olympic festival, as Hippias, Gorgias, and the Sophists had done in earlier times, in accordance with the idea that there should be open competition in every art and exercise. Gorgias's Pythian oration in particular was renowned in its treatment of the subject of Hellenic Unity, reminding one of our own great advocate's plea for Union under the Constitution. In the *Olympiacus* of Lysias the same thought is enforced of the political unity of Hellas against the barbarian. The funeral oration ascribed to Lysias, whether spoken by him or not, is another example of the demonstrative speech, which was celebrated in Aristotle's time, as was also the *Epitaphius* of Gorgias.

A prolongation of the form of Greek eloquence, after the departure of the spirit of liberty from it, tended to produce many orations which re-echoed the former eloquence and revived old issues, or invented less important topics for discussion. So in Rome, as there was at first an oratory which dealt with momentous questions until these began to be settled by imperial absolutism, there also followed a period when men who could speak found that they must confine themselves to subjects of a general nature. No doubt, in these periods of declining freedom, the occasional oration, dealing with harmless generalities, abounded; but it was composed under such restrictions, and in such a lifeless or corrupt style, that it could have only a brief existence. Such ephemeral productions vanished, with a hundred other fungi, in the general decay of the declining empire.

For centuries after the fifth it is difficult to find forensic or deliberative or much demonstrative oratory outside ecclesiastical precincts. The pulpit in the church or market-place or open field has a monopoly of eloquence, in a style which varied with the place and the man, and sometimes included the demonstrative phase, if not the judicial and deliberative, in court and council.   As it may be safely asserted that there were many eulogies spoken, so it may be inferred that many subjects of a general character were unfolded. Great events were commemorated, and important anniversaries were celebrated by clerical orators—the coronation of kings, the institution of orders, the consecration of bishops, the founding of religious houses, the dedication of temples, sacred and secular.   There was all the greater need of the occasional orator in the ages when oral communication of knowledge was the only method of reaching multitudes who could not read and had nothing to read. In the meantime there was no printer's art to preserve what might have been worth preserving, nor any reporter who could put into manuscript whatever might be worth saving.   A few written sermons have survived the general destruction, but they belong mostly to the distinct branch of homiletic oratory.

It is long after the revival of letters that what may be called the occasional oration, outside the eulogy, begins to appear in literature. A few instances in the reign of Louis Fourteenth, on the occasion of some royal or ecclesiastical solemnity, a few more apostrophes to learning or liberty in later ages, some stated academic performances in the universities of the continent and in England are about all that can be excavated from the literary accumulations of the renaissance centuries. They are chiefly valuable as signs and tokens of what was current in their age rather than as instructive examples for our own. Not much will be lost if they are passed over, and we come directly to our own century and country where abundant examples may be found of what is most needed in the study of the memorial address.

It may seem to be an unpardonable oversight to pass by the eloquence of Great Britain in the last century without enumerating at length examples of commemorative speech; but the overwhelming mass of deliberative oratory, supplemented by forensic argumentation, nearly hide the remnant that may be called occasional. Of this a number of eulogistic instances have been already cited under the appropriate title.

For the rest, the civil and ecclesiastical records furnish abundant material that has had a local and temporary interest and value.

There is no lack of this kind of discourse in our own land and literature.   In the same col-

In America. lection where so many examples of the eulogy are found there is a similar abundance of commemorative orations. Beginning with those of an academic character: there is a volume containing perhaps only a hundredth part of all that have been delivered; but in these eighteen chance specimens there are addresses to alumni associations by Joseph Story, Robert C. Winthrop, Henry J. Raymond, and Nicholas Biddle.   This collection, it should be said, is aside from the Phi Beta Kappa anniversary addresses at many colleges in many years, which themselves constitute a small library.   Here anticipatory mention may be made of three notable addresses which were made in commemoration of the founding of as many universities; that of President Barnas Sears on the one hundreth anniversary of the founding of Brown University in 1867; that of James Russell Lowell on the two hundred and fiftieth anniversary of the founding of Harvard University in 1886; and that of Grover Cleveland, President of the United States, on the two hundredth anniversary of the founding of Princeton University in 1896. There are also four volumes of anniversary discourses, mostly by ministers, and thirteen volumes of centennial discourses, in which the settlement of one town or city after another is celebrated, not to mention at length Jeremy Belknap's commemoration of the discovery of America (1792), or John Quincy Adams's (1843) on the New England Confederacy of 1643. Ralph Waldo Emerson and John Gorham Palfrey did not hesitate to follow, in 1835, and 1839, respectively, upon a lesser theme, as John Hancock had spoken in 1739 upon no greater theme than the Settlement of Braintree. Seventeen volumes of election sermons, four hundred and seventy-five in all, testify to the importance which early republicanism had in New England. The Fourth of July has already inspired eight volumes of addresses deemed worthy of publication, two hundred and twenty-five in number, besides sixty-five delivered in Boston which have also found their way into print. It should be borne in mind that this collection is only one out of many that are in existence, and that a complete list of all that have been spoken or printed, would itself make a volume of no inconsiderable size. Enough, however, have been cited to show that the literature of the commemorative address in this country is extensive. It is also creditable. Compared with contemporaneous efforts in other depart-ments of literature the oration does not suffer. To emphasize this statement it may be well to cite examples which best illustrate this branch of oratory.

As has been observed, there were instances of commemorative speech from the first settle-ment of New England; but it was *Webster's commemora-tive orations.* just two hundred years from the landing at Plymouth before the per-fected flower of eloquence blossomed in the commemorative discourse of Daniel Webster, recalling the virtues of the pilgrims and review-ing the growth of the State they founded. It is one of the greater achievements of a great orator. With calm and philosophic survey he traces the course of a new empire from its obscure fountain in a Yorkshire village—a few families escaping in a stormy night to a desolate coast, and in a frail craft crossing the North Sea to a foreign land, more hospitable than their own, where they waited for another removal to the bleak wilderness across the Atlantic.   The colonial life of the new country is then compared with that of other people and times; its marvellous prosperity, its independence, its devotion to learning and religion, its public spirit, wise legislation, love of literature, all contributing to make a nation exceptional in the advantages which it affords for the development of what is best in human life and character.   Five years later the address delivered at the laying of the corner-stone of the Bunker Hill Monument presented another example of what the new nation could produce in the way of demonstrative eloquence.   It was a memorial of a struggle for liberty, as the other was a commemoration of the planting of a new people.   As such a memorial it recalled the scenes enacted on that consecrated Hill fifty years before, in which the little group of venerable men before the speaker had taken part. His address to them and to their comrades who fell in battle as if present, is worthy of the epitaphian eloquence of the best Hellenic orators or of the eulogists of Louis Fourteenth's reign. His encomium of Lafayette has all the grace without the qualifications of Pliny's address to Trajan. Following this is the account of cordial sympathy and co-operation which made thirteen separate colonies one in purpose and action, with a review of the prosperity which had attended the first half century of the nation's existence. Its advance in wealth and knowledge, the sciences and the arts are portrayed with vividness and power. The consequent obligations of a free and prosperous people are not forgotten, and the duty of defence and preservation is enforced with words of courage and hope, '' that the country itself may become a vast and splendid Monument of Wisdom, Peace, and Liberty.''

The next year Mr. Webster delivered the most eloquent of all the memorial addresses which were pronounced throughout the land on the death of Adams and Jefferson, fifty years from the Declaration of Independence. It was an occasion which was its own inspiration, conveying its own lesson; but this great orator was the man to interpret it to his contemporaries in the old Cradle of Liberty, full of historic memories. The key-note of his masterly eulogium is the sentiment, that though dead they live to their country in their imperishable work for that country.

"Like the benignity of a summer's day, they have gone down with slow-descending, grateful, long-lingering light to cheer with good omens from beyond the visible margin of the world."

Similarities in the lives and fortunes of these great men are then traced, and afterward an account of the life of each is given in bold outline. The point where they converge and mingle in the Declaration of Independence is made the occasion for noting the part each bore in this momentous proceeding—the one drawing up and the other defending the charter of American liberties promulgated by the new nation for itself, to be established by its own arms, and sealed with its own blood. The merits of Jefferson's noble Composition are emphasized, while Adams's advocacy of it is made the inspiration of the famous definition of eloquence beginning: " When public bodies are to be addressed on momentous occasions," and ending with the assertion that " it is something greater than eloquence; it is action, noble, sublime, godlike action." Contemporaneous testimony asserts that the speaker himself was the best illustration of his statement. In the speech which he attributes to Adams, notwithstanding its dramatic fidelity, there is much of Mr. Webster's own personality. The words " Sink or swim, live or die, survive or perish," have a pre-revolutionary tone; but the imputed sentiments are such as the eulogist himself would have uttered had he lived in that period which tried men's souls.

After a tribute to the zealous attachment of both to the cause of sound learning, which their own lives and characters illustrated, passing judiciously over controversies which belonged to the administration of each, he gathers up the instruction of two illustrious lives, and enforces the obligation of following such worthy examples.

"This lovely land, this glorious liberty, these benign institutions are ours; ours to enjoy, ours to preserve, ours to transmit. Let not the blood of the fathers have been shed in vain; the great hope of posterity, let it not be blasted. Beneath the illumination of our own stars in the firmament let us walk the course of life, and at its close commend our beloved country to the Divine Benignity."

In 1843, eighteen years from the laying of the corner-stone, Mr. Webster delivered the address of dedication of Bunker Hill Monument. It is marked by the same nobleness of sentiment and grace of diction that characterized the first address, and conveys the same lessons of devoted patriotism. The two together doubtless did much to inspire that generation and the succeeding one with loyalty to the Union and with gratitude to the founders and defenders of national liberty. These, and the Plymouth oration will remain pre-eminent as master-pieces of commemorative eloquence. Their best passages have been learned by the lads of three generations, and their sound political teachings have been absorbed with the studies of the schools; contributing in no small degree to good citizenship and patriotism throughout the land. Great judicial arguments and greater deliberative speeches were made by Mr. Web-,

ster and his contemporaries, but it is his un-
equalled achievements in demonstrative oratory
that have been the educators of the people in
the principles of constitutional freedom.   How
much they have done also in forming a sound
taste in public speech can be estimated only by
probabilities; but it is safe to say, that his
sturdy Anglo-Saxon vocabulary, his vigorous
diction, strong in the power of the common
word rightly placed, dependent for its effectiveness upon no fanciful arrangement or far-
fetched device, his sustained discourse, moving
always with imperial dignity and apparent ease,
contributed largely to the character of public
speech in the age succeeding his own.   The
best of this is not widely diverse from its great
exemplar.   It could not be without unfavorable
comparison with the people's standard.   Other
orators might have more classic elegance, more
vivid imagination, more sparkling wit, more of
the spoils of antiquity, and more graceful flexi-
bility, but none more of strong sense, profound
reason, and weighty diction.   Nor were any
endowed with the irresistible force of his ma-
jestic presence, which is said to have towered

like a mountain over his hearers.   Aside from these efforts Mr. Webster did not deliver many commemorative addresses or turn much away from professional and senatorial duties.   These few examples, however, show that he was equal to the greatest occasions.

The orator who made the occasional address almost the vocation of his life was Edward Everett.   In his works, evidently published under his immediate supervision, six orations out of the first seven are commemorative in character.   The first of these is at Plymouth, two years after Webster's, the next at Concord, another at Cambridge, two more at Charlestown, and the sixth at the erection of a monument to John Harvard.   All these were delivered within the first four years of his public life.   Others follow at an interval of about a year between them,—orations and speeches signalizing some occurrence; eulogies and memorial addresses commemorating one event or life and another. The entire collection constitutes almost a branch of American literature in itself.   Based upon classic foundations these productions might pass for the work of an Attic orator if they had been rendered into the Greek language,—as this eminent scholar could have rendered them if he had chosen. There were allusions in them which would have been at home in the Greek tongue and country, while the liberty he lauded and inculcated would have harmonized with Hellenic discourse. " Olympia " closes the first paragraph of his first oration, " Panegyric of Isocrates " occurs on the first page of it, and few leaves can be turned in any address without betraying his familiarity with ancient oratorical literature and his fondness for what is best and noblest in it. On a page which happens to lie open the first words are " Homer and Cicero," and within a little more than its extent is a comparison of the literatures of the Alexandrian and Periclean ages, of the Roman and the Italian, of Dante, Boccacio, and Petrarch; of Spanish, French, and English writers. Tasso, Cervantes, Corneille, Shakespeare, Milton, Johnson, Burke, and many another are cited to show of how little value is the patronage of letters by governments. Following these orations were others upon " The Boyhood and Youth of Franklin," " The Second Century of Harvard College," a " Eulogy on John Adams," " The Battle of Bunker Hill," " The Dedication of Boston Public Library."   Other notable addresses are those upon Benjamin Franklin, Daniel Webster, Washington Irving, " The Vindication of American Institutions," " Causes and Conduct of the Civil War," and " The National Cemetery at Gettysburg."   In addition to these there were short speeches on public occasions when Mr. Everett's absence would have been counted as something wanting to the completeness of the arrangements. The entire collection of his occasional addresses fills five large volumes, giving him the precedence, if not the primacy, so far as numbers go, among the occasional orators of this century, and, perhaps, in all centuries.

18

III.

THE EXPOSITORY ADDRESS.

I T is with Edward Everett also that a type of
the occasional address became prominent
which can be considered as more general in
character than either the eulogy or commemorative oration, its purpose being to
set forth or interpret the suggested
topic of the hour.   The subject
itself may belong to the wide domain of general truths and principles, and the object of the
speaker may be equally large and comprehensive.   Occasions will arise of a literary, social,
or civil nature which demand appropriate celebration or recognition without the necessary
discussion of a " burning question of the hour,"
and when such discussion would be entirely
out of place and foreign to the spirit of the
occasion.   There might be a violation of the

Exposition
and interpre-
tation.

social compact in bringing the neediest of causes before the audience.   The orator's object at such a time may be no more defined than to meet the demand for a speaker who shall help to secure an hour of good feeling, peace, and harmony among a great assembly of people having diverse interests and dispositions, opinions, and beliefs.   Indeed, one who shall induce such a symphony of souls for an hour has, for that space of time, accomplished 'the end and purpose of all laudable speech and labor towards anticipating the millennium.   It is because such desirable states are not yet permanent that more aggressive words and more violent action are resorted to in order to hasten the coming of the kingdom which mankind always believes is in the future.   It is therefore no ignoble undertaking to make of one heart and one mind even a hundred hearers for as many minutes.

The power to do this and the way to do it were both exemplified in the oratory of Mr. Everett on numerous occasions.   A man of peace himself, he was an orator to speak peace to either discordant or

Edward
Everett.

harmonious assemblies.   Signal examples of this conciliatory tone of address were the three speeches delivered on the occasion of public festivities as he was travelling through Tennessee, Kentucky, and Ohio the year after his memorial address upon John Harvard. The Union is the burden of his thought, and the increasing confederation of States extending itself westward with prosperity assured in the fertile fields of a new country. No note of possible antagonism or rival interests was uttered on an "occasion consecrated to the oblivion of every topic of party strife." A projected National Road was to bind the States together; the news of the battle of Lexington in Massachusetts had given the name to the capital of Kentucky; and this was in the "era of good feeling," which no one did more to promote than the peace-loving advocate of harmony, even at the expense of subserviency to sectional domination in politics, as some thought. A discourse on the "Importance of Scientific Knowledge to Practical Men" is another example of a theme of general application. The diffusion of useful knowledge among the working classes, the improvement of their minds, and the consequent elevation above things altogether sordid, was a subject in which the large benevolence and profound learning of the speaker found an opportunity to mingle for the general welfare without disturbing the prejudices of many hearers.   There is a pleasant wholesomeness about such discourse which commends itself to a mixed multitude of skilled mechanics, who are not without their fixed opinions and ready criticisms, but, as the speaker remarked, " never vicious or indolent as a class."   Before these he held up the example of the world's great workers, many of them men of genius.   An essential part of this he showed to consist in the capacity and disposition for persistent and persevering toil.

It may be surprising to those who know of Mr. Everett chiefly by traditions of his classic stateliness, that he could thus interest the masses.   One who knew him well and heard him often once wrote:

" Because he was naturally reserved and shy, and took no pains to invite a following of the young men of his day, they in turn took on a critical tone in speaking of him which has

been continued to the present time. It is easier to call him
' frigid and artificial, priggish and pedantic ' than to account
for those qualities to which his contemporaries cordially bear
witness ; qualities which in some way made his audiences take
the roof off in their wild enthusiasm when he led them up
and on as hardly any other speaker I have ever seen. He had
extraordinary power in absolutely extemporary discourse more
than any man I ever knew."

The fact that he trained no school of followers,
should in no degree qualify an eloquence which
it is easier to dispute than to rival.

Rufus Choate was another master of the interpretative address.   Amidst the occupations
of an extremely crowded professional
life he found time for the cultivation
of literature, and for the exposition of its best
lessons to the people.   As indicating the range
of his studies may be cited the titles of his
addresses on " The Importance of Illustrating
New England History by a Series of Ro-
mances," " The Colonial Age of New England," " The Heroic Period of Our History,"
" The Power of a State Developed by Mental
Culture," " The Eloquence of Revolutionary
Periods," " The Position of the American Bar
as an Element of Conservatism in the State,"
and " Amercan Nationality."   To these may

be added " A Discourse Commemorative of Daniel Webster," delivered at Dartmouth College, the *alma mater* of both Mr. Webster and Mr. Choate.

It was with Mr. Everett and Mr. Choate that the occasional address sometimes passed into the form of the popular lecture, itself to assume an important place in the more general education of the **The popular lecture and lecturers.** people.   Combining entertainment with instruction, it became a field into which entered the best literary and oratorical ability of the nation for a period of forty years.   Every Northern city had several courses each winter, and every town of considerable importance secured such talent as it could afford.   Churches, lyceums, and speculators went into the lecture business for the good of the community, and incidentally for the emolument of the parties undertaking it.   But, strictly speaking, the lecture was not an occasional address, as it was not mainly didactic.   Often it did interpret some truth, or discuss a question of morals, politics, or philosophy; but the occasion was almost as frequent and regular as the

Sunday, and the subject had sometimes the flavor and treatment of a sermon. Like homiletic literature, that of the lecture was generally ephemeral, and is largely lost or scattered in biographies and collected works of one and another of its once famous authors. Of these, among the best known at the height of the lecture period were Chapin, Beecher, Gough, Emerson, Phillips, Curtis, and Holmes. With the departure of these men, the glory of the popular lecture passed away. Strenuous endeavors were made here and there to preserve its usefulness and power, but with little success. It had come and gone with the orators and the issues that grew into importance together, and with the increasing thoughtfulness of a people who listened to the speakers and meditated upon their presentation of momentous questions. When these were settled the surviving lecturers themselves found little stimulus in subordinate themes, and the people, relieved from a protracted strain, turned to lighter diversions or plunged into special and technical studies.

Charles Sumner added to his eulogistic and commemorative orations already mentioned others of an interpretative character, as, for example, the lectures on the "Employment of Time," on "Slavery and the Mexican War," "White Slavery in the Barbary States," "Fame and Glory," "The Law of Human Progress." These are but a small fraction of his declarations on similar themes; but such utterances were largely in the United States Senate, or before political meetings. His speeches and addresses are those of a statesman, although upon occasions of a literary character he was surpassed by few.

Robert C. Winthrop began his public career with occasional addresses upon "The Pilgrim Fathers," "The Influence of Commerce," "The National Monument to Washington," "Free Schools and Free Governments," and "The Bible." Then his congressional life began, and speeches and remarks are the rule with him rather than the more formal occasional address. Memorable exceptions are the addresses on "The Obligations and Responsibilities of Educated Men"; an address at the laying of the corner-stone of Boston Public Library, 1855, and another at its dedication, 1858; on the ⸙ Two Hundred and Fiftieth Anniversary of the Landing of the Pilgrims ''; an oration on '' Colonel William Prescott,'' at Bunker Hill; another, at Yorktown, Virginia, on '' Cornwallis's Surrender,'' and another at the unveiling of the statue of Daniel Webster in New York, and the '' Centennial Oration '' in Boston, 1876.

Wendell Phillips's contributions to the literature of the expository address can best be known by an examination of his works. His public life was filled with such addresses, many of which he passed as lectures upon willing audiences. '' Public Opinion,'' '' The Pilgrims,'' '' Idols,'' '' The Lost Arts,'' '' Disunion,'' '' Progress,'' '' The Education of the People,'' '' The Scholar in a Republic,'' are examples of themes which he developed for the instruction of his fellow-citizens in their manifold duties. In these subjects and through them often ran the current of his antagonism to slavery, and in some of them this was the main thought and purpose; but aside from this he had much to say to his listeners about a wide variety of truths. How

wide, a reading of the addresses themselves
will best show.

Ralph Waldo Emerson found the lecture
platform a movable bema from which he
uttered things not heard in the pul- Ralph Waldo
pits of his forefathers for seven gen-   Emerson.
erations.   But such was the charm of his voice
and personality that his sphinx-like, oracular
epigrams delighted listeners.   What they could
not understand they called heresy, and what
they did not believe they supposed to be
transcendentalism, and invited him to come
again the next winter.

George William Curtis was another who was
a clear interpreter of events and affairs as they
succeeded one another in the stirring
times before and after the Civil War.   George
William
By pen and tongue he made plain   Curtis.
the duty of American patriots and philanthro-
pists, of citizens and scholars.   It was his good
fortune to be able to do this through influen-
tial journals as well as on the platform, and in
himself to represent a transition of literary
effort from the latter to the former, which took
place in the last quarter of the century.

Taken together, the second and third quarters of it produced a group of orators who illustrate the value of the expository and interpretative address as a public educator in life, letters, and politics beyond any former company of speakers in modern times. There have been coteries of great orators who were advocates, statesmen, and preachers; but for men who combine with their professional ability the versatility and broad culture that enables them to explore and reveal other fields of knowledge, the group just mentioned stands pre-eminent if not supreme.

IV.

THE COMMENCEMENT ORATION.

FOR two hundred and fifty years this form of the occasional address has been the most familiar, because the most frequent one in this country.   At each academic anniversary there has usually been delivered a Its literature abundant. learned and somewhat stately pro- duction by a distinguished speaker before some association.   The entire collection of such addresses form a literature unsurpassed in volume for profundity of erudition and elegance of expression.   One has only to inquire at any college library for as much of this as he will need to peruse to get into the current of thought and style in any year of the last two centuries. He will find many notable examples of eloquence and wisdom which are worth reading for their practical value, and as examples of the English style prevailing at the time. Some of them are the best fruit of culture in their respective generations. The oration of the graduating student is, however, the main topic in this chapter. That it is a subject worth considering may be inferred from the fact that there are about as many colleges in the land as there are days in the year. Allowing the usual number of speakers to each graduating class, there cannot be less than three thousand orations delivered during the annual Commencement season. Counting professional schools, this number will be greatly increased.

In this computation a small deduction may be made for the universities which have grown **Its probable** to such dimensions that Commence-**permanence.** ment exercises must consist in functions belonging to university rather than to collegiate affairs. But the numerical ratio of students in the Amerian college has not so greatly increased in the last half-century as to justify a demand for general change in the time-honored method of closing the academic year. Eight colleges in New England, for instance, average but a little over two hundred students each; and although there have been many changes in matters of instruction and equipment, there appears to be little need to discard the representation of the college by speakers on Commencement Day, and little likelihood that this custom will be discontinued for some time to come. Not because it is a venerable custom, nor because colleges are conservative; but because the community, and especially the alumni, have a natural desire to know what a college is doing for its students, as indicated by their performance on the only day in the year when they appear in public in a literary character. It will be an evil day for any college when, without good and sufficient reason, it is unwilling to submit to this test of the work its pupils are doing, or when the students themselves are unwilling.

In regard to the oration itself, let the above remark suggest the first condition of it, namely, that it should be representative in character. The objection sometimes urged, that these academic productions are not of great value in themselves, has nothing to do with the question of abolishing them altogether. Many sermons, and other addresses, fall under the same condemnation ; but all preaching and public speaking are not on this account to be done away with. Moreover, people do not attend Commencements to be instructed, although it may be said that they do sometimes get more than they look for. Their chief interest in a speaker, aside from a personal interest, is to observe what present methods of education have done for the graduates of any year, as shown in a fair presentation of it by the best of the class, as other bodies are represented by their best. Therefore it will be the first thought of the Commencement speaker to see that he adequately represents his college in his day.

Accordingly he will not begin to look for a topic among the programmes of former years.

Subject should be interesting. There is no particular interest in themes which were full of suggestivenesss a hundred years ago. Such as " The French Revolution," or " The Importance of Encouraging Genius," or " The

Comparative Advantages of the Civilized and Savage State"; "The Happiness of America"; "The Importance of Education to a Republican Government"; "Anticipation as Preferable to Enjoyment"; "The Superiority of Agriculture to Other Arts"; "The Bad Effects of Party in a State." All these themes, taken from programmes yellow with the dust of a hundred years, have an ancient and musty flavor about them, suggesting the infancy of our Republic, and of American letters. In a similar category may be classed certain abstruse philosophical and metaphysical subjects often supposed to be of universal and eternal interest because perennially interesting to students in the last year of their college course, when they pursue such studies. They should be sparingly introduced into any Commencement list, and mainly to satisfy the demand of a department. This, however, is only a single phase of the larger temptation to which graduating students are subject—that is, the desire to discuss in public, as they have discussed in class, the scholastic themes of their senior year. As has been remarked, such presentation will doubtless show what their proficiency is, and perhaps this is all that an audience has a right to expect; but the speaker must not suppose that one tenth of his hearers are going to be interested in this sort of themes. If he is debating whether to write of things scholastic, fresh in his own mind, or of things occupying the popular mind, the latter will be safe. A subject of present interest need not be rejected because the speaker cannot say anything new or the last word about it. And if the pleasure of the audience be taken into account, and their consequent attention, it will be better to choose a theme appropriate to the beginning of a new century than to go back to earlier decades; to speak, for instance, of currency questions rather than of the Missouri Compromise; or again, of " New Methods in Criminology " than of " The Limits of the Conditioned." Of all the topics which a speaker can appropriately select, possibly one which presents valuable or inspiring instruction in a personal form is safest to choose; linking it with the character and life of a man not too generally known, but who has made an honorable place for him-

self by worthy if not conspicuous attainment.
Such examples are often full of interest and
encouragement, and afford opportunity to
clothe abstract truth in attractive garb. On
the other hand, there is no subject however
abstruse which cannot be made clear and interesting if the writer knows how to make it so.

Treatment, then, will perhaps be of more
consequence in some instances than choice of
subject.   This is not saying that Treatment of
style is of more value than thought.   theme.
It is the prolonged, patient, and therefore the
eventually clear thought that is the next obligation of the Commencement orator.   Misty
rumination, clothed in ambiguous and vague
phraseology does not pass for profoundity because uttered in the dialect of erudition.   The
higher the theme, the simpler and plainer
should be the diction, and the more illuminating the figures of speech.

In these thought processes it will accordingly
be of the greatest value if they can be made to
crystallize around two or three defi-   Making
nite points.   It is a frequent charac-   points.
teristic of academic orations that they exhibit

a uniformity of production from beginning to end. They lack the variety of emphasis. They are apt to be a series of statements instead of a cumulative treatment of a few propositions ending in points so clearly made that the listener cannot escape them. Points, too, are all that he can be expected to remember; the fewer and stronger the better. Perhaps one point, well made, is enough; if so, let it be approached by a diversified path rather than on the uniform level of a railway track. If more than one are attempted let them be made so few and plain that they will not be forgotten when the topic and the speaker are remembered. Generally it is the impression only, good or poor, that can be carried away after several have spoken.

Another tendency in preparation is to undertake too much for a ten-minute speech. It is not borne in mind that an audience **Condensation and compression.** does not expect a speaker to tell all he knows, and to give the total result of a four-years' course of study in a thousand words. To be sure, it is not an easy task to compress all that can be said upon an interesting topic within these limits and do it justice. This is not demanded. All that is wanted is to see what the speaker might do if he had more time. It is the few paces that show the gait, the few minutes the man, the few men the college. The speaker who has spoken ten minutes may be sure that his hearers will credit him with much more than he has had time to say, and for more knowledge than he has exhibited. Condensation will be of value. No one knows the compressibility of thought and of language so well as those who are limited in the space and time at their command. Condensation is the student's bane, the last accomplishment he acquires. " How can I condense these twenty pages into ten ? " asked a pupil. " An easy matter," replied the professor, " paste them together." The result could doubtless have been accomplished more satisfactorily by cutting down each sentence to its essential length and without the loss of a single thought. It is the qualification of statements and their needless fortification that most often fill the page and tire the listener.

After blocking out and clearing up the

thought, absorbing or rejecting such material as has been gathered in preparation, there will

Technical terms to be avoided. be some choice in the kind of diction to be employed when much is to be said in a short time. The natural propensity is to fly to technical terms with their precise comprehensiveness. This will do in some places and with some hearers. In an academic audience it is a nice question about the currency of scholastic terms. The faculty will understand them; the graduating class, if they have all elected the subject; those of the alumni who have not forgotten it, and sundry ambitious readers, constituting all together perhaps one third the average Commencement audience. The orator or his instructor must decide whether it is better not to be understood by the other two thirds than to lose time in making a technical subject clear by circumlocutory phrases. It is not so grave a fault to use the technical term as if the audience before him were a political one. Even there also can be found technical terms, and who but the initiated can understand the lingo of athletics, or for that matter all the English of the college precincts ?   Still the benevolent speaker will be " altruistic " enough to remember that in the " solidarity " before him there are some who have no more " cognition " of his meaning when he indulges in the abstruse terminology of the classroom than when he is sporting the dialect of the ball-field or of the college grounds.   He will therefore try to speak English as it is understood by the greatest number on all occasions—Commencement-Day among the rest.

The desire and the necessity to condense may betray the writer of an oration into a fault of diction indicated by the word " choppy."   Epigrammatic sentences, containing the gist of whole paragraphs, and following one another without apparent connection, cannot carry the meaning of ten times their volume, for which the speaker finds he has no room.   This may do for the essayist's printed page, when the reader has time to construct bridges from one isolated dictum to another.   But the hearer has not this advantage.   Accordingly, the only resource left to the speaker is to give a reasonable fulness to his diction, and not undertake to exhaust his subject. He will lay off a small plat for thorough tillage rather than stake out acres to ramble over.

For this reason he will better attempt something in the line of a thesis than the conventional oration. This is indeed the best form of an academic production for the Commencement stage. It does not require the oratorical construction and expression, to which students are naturally averse on account of their inexperience and the limited time allowed for speaking. It is, moreover, the form in which a thorough exposition of one segment of a general subject can be presented or a single proposition be maintained. Furthermore, it has the sanction of antiquity, from the time when students presented their theses for degrees in mediæval universities, and it is to-day the customary graduating exercise in professional schools, and in one at least of the larger universities lately established. In method, it develops a single point of a subject as fully as time will allow, without undertaking to trace all the ramifications. It may thus be scholarly without pedantry, and interesting without an attempt at eloquence or elocution.

By this it is not intended to cast any slight upon good delivery.   This part of the address needs more attention, rather than less, as the composition becomes less **Delivery.** oratorical in character, or the place less favorable to elocutionary exhibition.   A good delivery is more difficult to acquire than good composition.   It is a natural gift, but one that may be wasted and lost or increased tenfold. Usually there is no lack of opportunity to make the most of one's ability in this direction while in college.   Still the conception of what is fitting in each speaker may vary, and other qualifications intervene to such an extent that it is only one in a hundred who meets with exceptional success.   A recent mistaken sentiment with regard to the value of a good delivery has also militated against vocal culture.   But a reaction is sure to come, and the human voice will once more be recognized as one of the highest endowments bestowed upon man for his influence over his fellows.   This gift, like other allotments, is not always placed where it will be most serviceable, nor is it always accompanied by due appreciation and cultivation on the part of the possessor; but conjoined with mental power and improved by training, a good vocalization is worth a fortune to a public speaker. As a surpassing accomplishment, however, the price of it is in long and faithful practice, and more tedious labor than most men are willing to bestow in these driving times. In college, if one half the time that is bestowed on other athletic exercise were given to vocal gymnastics, the effect would be as creditable to the college on Commencement days, as is the ball game. The results in improved health would also be no less than in other forms of exercise, without the dangers attendant upon some of them, and with more value in after-life.

It would be more agreeable, no doubt, to read directions for writing an effective oration, if they could be given here at length,

Methods of composition outlined. but such details belong to college courses in composition. Matters of choosing a subject, extracting a theme, finding first what one can himself say about it, and then what others have said, making notes of reading, distributing material in proper order, keeping the divisions distinct from each other, and separate points in mind, making the plan and filling it in, writing the first draft, revising, condensing, abridging, omitting,—all this is the daily work of one who expects to become an effective speaker. Something, too, will be caught from acquaintance with the literature of oratory, and something more from such suggestions as instructors may give. Chiefly, however, the good writer and speaker will be self-made. No amount of instruction will make a good mathematician out of a poor head for figures, or a poet out of a person in whom there is not an inborn aptitude for rhyme and metre. Neither can it be expected that one who has not the literary faculty will attain eminence in letters, or that one who has not the oratorical gifts will sway listening crowds. But it should be within the power of almost any educated man to state clearly and definitely whatever thoughts or information he may have upon ordinary subjects. According to his talents he should be able to do this upon the day of his graduation, if asked.   It is a duty he owes to his college, and to the men who have endowed it.   Possibly he owes it to those who have given him golden opportunities of education.   If he has earned these by his own efforts he owes it to himself to take advantage of every occasion which shall place him before an assembly of his fellow-men, as one who has a message from his *alma mater* to the community in which it stands as an uplifting force.   It may be for him the first of a series of messages which he shall utter in after life. It will be a help to him then if he make a creditable beginning now, as many distinguished men have made, on the day of their graduation.   Certainly he will seldom find an occasion more trying, or again, hearers more appreciative and charitable and attentive than on the day when he delivers his Commencement oration.

V.

THE POLITICAL SPEECH.

THIS chapter is not intended for veterans. They have learned things which it is not necessary to tell them; things which would be of great value if they could be recorded here for the benefit of the less experienced. It is this class that is addressed, with the remembrance fresh of a campaign year in college days. A few students, full of zeal for the party with which they had just cast their first municipal vote, had been **Students in a political campaign.** promised chances to speak before the impending election took place. It was a rare opportunity to put in practice rhetorical and oratorical theories they had learned in college. They also possessed some partisan enthusiasm which they called patriotism, and they had a share of that self-confidence which helps one to take

sanguine views.   Like Archimedes they said,
" Give us where to stand," although in justice
it must be added that they did not promise to
move the world.   But there were country vil-
lages not far away which had suffered many
things from student preachers, and it was
hoped that they would not despise similar performances of a political character.   Accordingly
vacation days were given to sundry theoretical
and practical studies in politics, preparatory to
stump speaking in the autumn.   It is not necessary to prolong the story of that campaign.
Results proved the supposition true, that there
is no better field for a collegian, or any young
man, to test the value of his knowledge, and
his estimate of his own powers and resources,
than in a political campaign.   He will learn
some things not taught in the schools, and become rapidly acquainted with human nature
and himself.   It may be worth the while to
mention a few particulars which readily trans-
late themselves into maxims of value to the
beginner in this kind of occasional oratory.

One of the first things he will discover is, the
unsuspected amount of information possessed

by an audience of ordinary people.   He does not recognize this latent knowledge as he looks them over.   He concludes that he is going to win an easy victory, if he can succeed in bringing his arguments down to the level of their intelligence. Getting under way with his speech, and wondering if he is talking over his hearers' heads, he may be interrupted with a question which all at once makes him doubt if he fully understands every side of his topic.   How did the knowledge requisite to ask that question get into this secluded town ?   He begins to suspect that somebody must take the other party's paper, which he himself has neglected to read on the supposition that all truth is the prerogative of his own party organs, and all political heresy the invention of opposition sheets. Furthermore, he is in a worse plight than his friend the divinity student, to whom the customary courtesy of the Sunday congregation permits no open cavil.   Not so is it in the campaign meeting; and if he succeed in replying satisfactorily to himself he may not to the satisfaction of the audience, and certainly will

not to that of the questioner. From this moment he will speak with the constant apprehension of further surprises. But they will do
him good if they spring up. They will teach
him that knowledge, like water, will leach into
remote places, and that under unpromising ap-
pearances there is often much shrewd sense
that cannot be overwhelmed by the best logic,
when convictions are backed by prejudice and
supposed interest. These last 'elements the
speaker will find conspicuously present when
he transfers his efforts from the country school-
house, or town-hall, to the ward room of the
city.

In either place he will learn one thing,
namely, that there is little delicacy and no

Value of con-
tact with
popular criti-
cism.

circumlocution or euphemism in
plain, blunt men who, like the
Athenian of old, consider themselves a part of the State because they cast
ballots. Their questions are challenges to be
met squarely, or with a frank confession of
their pertinency and merits. Their value to
the speaker is in setting him to dig about the
foundations of his belief, and to look for the

weak places in the oratorical and logical fabric he has been constructing for himself and the good of the country. Incidentally, also, he learns to be interrupted, and meanwhile to keep his temper and self-possession. Advocates acquire this useful habit in the courts, and legislators in assemblies; but it sometimes happens that when they are out of the arenas where combat is according to rule, they meet with an unconventional foe whose uncouth ways play the mischief with forensic and parliamentary methods. Defeat at such hands is not suggestive óf Waterloo so much as of Lexington. The '' embattled farmers' '' intermittent and galling fire is more annoying than the volleys of the regulars. To become accustomed to this ambuscade warfare, to learn to take as well as to give, is another acquisition of great value. Much depends upon good humor in this, for a lost temper is an argument lost. It betrays a distrust of one's strength and ability to defend his cause. A good-natured admission of fallibility is a thousand-fold better than petulant chagrin. He is an unarmed campaigner who has not always in expectation the adverse possibilities of the contest. The greatest of modern captains was always thinking not of what he should do when victorious, but of what way to escape the consequences of defeat.

Another precept, which is worth more than at first it seems to be worth, is regarding fair-

Fairness in discussion. ness toward the opposite party and rival candidates. The maxim " all is fair in war " is an easy one to apppropriate in political contests, and seemingly justifiable. Ethics are not supposed to enter into such warfare. Strong convictions must be inspired, and strong methods are requisite. The average political gathering is not likely to have the keenest sense of honorable methods. It appreciates success more than any means of winning it. Assertion, backed by the similitude of logic, but better by a pointed anecdote at the expense of the other side, is as good an argument as any for a crowd which is running with the speaker. But if the multitude is a mixed one, and there are voters to be conciliated and won from the opposition, the wise speaker will make a show at least of treating their preconceptions with fairness. He will in this way secure a more favorable hearing when he comes to the statement of his own side. In the great political campaign debate between Stephen A. Douglas and Abraham Lincoln, the fairness of the latter toward his. opponent did as much for his ultimate success as what he said for his own side. Frank generosity disarms prejudice and paves the way for an honest presentation of unpalatable considerations. Still, there is abundant opportunity for discretion here. There is no call for a ruinous generosity. Political wisdom suggests a benevolence toward the opposing side in minor matters, or in undeniable facts, rather than in those radical differences upon which the greater questions turn.

Akin to this is the sharp practice of making the most of an adversary's weak points, and thus diverting attention from one's Making most own. It is a ruse of the bar and the of diversions. battle-field, and has been known to do yeoman service on the political platform. If its legitimate result can be immediately secured it will have its own reward. But if there be time for the public press to arraign such methods, their efficiency will be neutralized by the exposure which they are sure to receive. In these days the speaker has it all his own way for an hour. Then he is brought before the people in their cooler moments and finds their judgment pronounced in advance by an interpreting press. With varying interpretation, to be sure, but it is not all in any one direction, as may have been the case in the wigwam of his tribe. Therefore it is of great importance that a speaker have a long outlook toward the merciless judgment which is sure to follow any wide departure from what is fair toward the opposition or from what is true of his own cause.

But it is entirely in accord with political ethics to say that a speaker on the political platform will do all that he can for his own side. This is expected of him. Up to the verge of the line which separates truth from falsehood, personalities from slander, exaggeration from misrepresentation, he will carry his assertions, and most men will think his method legitimate. It will be credited to his belief in his cause and

Support of speaker's own cause.

his devotion to it. A judicial spirit might be taken for indifference and half-heartedness: a concessive temper for trimming and temporizing. It is the last place to show any other than a positive and zealous committal of mind and heart to the doctrines and purposes of the party. Its way is, without doubt, the one way; its triumph the only hope of the community, of the state, of society, of the age, and of humanity.

To carry such strong personal convictions there will be need of strong language. This can be very strong. It will be full of those potent nouns, verbs, and idiomatic phrases which the people understand without a dictionary, the Saxon words they use when they are excited. Expletives which are not profane will sometimes creep in, but circumlocutions never, unless for ridicule. Characterization will be with a broad and free stroke, like the charcoal sketch of a master, something that the dullest can see and comprehend, as they might comprehend a caricature of Nast's. Clear division, like that of the oration, will be doubly valuable here when

the audience is mixed, untrained, and unrestrained.   Points must be made, barbed points
that will fix themselves in undisciplined minds.
Therefore words will be sharp and short, not
hard to recall.   Current and new phrases are
admissible here more than elsewhere.

One advantage the political speaker has over
all other orators,—he must speak, without a
sign of manuscript or not speak at
all.   Nothing could be more incongruous than a written stump speech.   The very
respectability of form is against it.   The spirit
of earnest address is hampered by such a token
of premeditation.   There should be sufficient
forethought, all the more that there are no
notes to rely upon; but the appearance should
be of spontaneous speech because the head and
heart are supposed to be full.   When they are
overflowing with zeal, exact, correct, and precise terms are not looked for.   Syntax can be
violated more safely than earnestness; rhythm
and movement than sincerity.   The one idea
will so possess the speaker that he is sublimely
unconscious of slips of tongue, and people will
forgive his mistakes by reason of his singleness

of purpose. He will not add to his verbal errors by going back to correct them. The correction is worse than the blunder; for it calls everybody's attention to what some would not have noticed and others would have soon forgotten.

Here, too, the value of extemporary speech will be evident in the opportunity it gives to meet emergencies as they arise. Not merely the interrupting interroga- Meeting emergencies. tories that have been mentioned, but changes in the temper of a crowd always fickle and centrifugal, ready to fly off in unexpected directions on the slightest provocation. The speaker who can ride out their shifting gales is fortunate; he who can direct the whirlwind is more fortunate still. The throng must not get away with the speaker; it is worse if they make head against him. But it is one of the crowning achievements of the orator to turn back a threatening herd, as Phillips turned them in Faneuil Hall and Curtis in Chicago. To do this is the prerogative of the man whose wits are about him, and who has left his notes at home. He must also have stores of knowledge upon which he can draw, and be able to think upon his feet.   He will need to break out new paths at short notice, to fight foes in ambush, to be armed at all points, and always to be in command of himself.   Otherwise he cannot rule the noise of the people and the madness of a multitude.

There are many places in which the speaker's prowess is tested, many trying situations, some The political which are more trying than they convention. seem, as in arguing a case before a committee or a board where the inspiration to eloquence is small.   In a political convention, on the other hand, there are the incitements of enthusiasm or even the goads of a hissing opposition; but all in all, there is no greater opportunity for signal success or ignominious failure.   It will be the one or the other that will receive attention, since mediocrity gets little notice.   Certainly no situation calls for all the faculties of the speaking man to be kept alert and in extreme tension more than when making the platform speech.   None requires more general preparation, not only for what is to be said, but also for what may be demanded by the other side. Comprehensive study of all sides of the questions at issue, shrewdness to anticipate points of attack, and a thorough acquaintance with lines of defence are the beginnings of success. But the ability to turn the tide of battle and divert the headlong rush of sentiment surging hither and thither, ready to precipitate itself into any ditch dug for the unwary; to control such a rout as is guided by the herdsman when he rounds up ramping cattle, is the privilege and the power of only here and there a man in a century. It has been done three or four times in the nineteenth: there are likely to be other opportunities in the twentieth. The madness of the people has not been permanently cured; nor, on the other hand, have they as yet shown themselves independent of the sway exercised by masters of assemblies.

The literature of this branch of the public address is not comparatively abundant because it is necessarily ephemeral. Burke's speech to the electors of Bristol is as far back as one need turn for a first-class production, and the doctrine there promulgated of the independence of the representative is a wholesome one for all political candidates to study. After this speech others may be sought among the works of statesmen, but often with little success; for it is the kind of effort to which they have been least willing to give immortality. Office has often been more creditable than the means necessary to obtain it. Furthermore the issues discussed have been of little importance, and the speeches themselves local and temporary in character, designed to win ballots and nothing more. Newspapers keep in the darkness and dust of their mouldy files the remains of much eloquence that once thrilled enthusiastic crowds. It was not unlike what may be heard in any exciting presidential campaign, a quadrennial flood which covers the land, and men predict a deluge of disaster and the extinction of the nation in consequence. When the waters subside they always find in some corner of the sky a bow of promise. After all, discussion is better than silence, and the information of the people than their ignorance. Therefore it is well that the platform should share with the press the burden of political education, never too thorough among a people politically inclined. But it is to the journalism of the country that we shall always be indebted for preserving the literature of the political platform. The making of it is the safety-valve of the Republic.

There may also be found in dark corners of libraries, public and private, copies of speeches that have been mailed from Washington regardless of expense—because there was none. Many times these are copies of speeches that have actually been delivered. In this case they must be reckoned among the literature of the campaign. Collectors of the curious here and there will have what has been worth keeping; but of it all it is no disparagement to say that its chief value consists in the delivery of it to an audience.

As confirming this opinion was the proclamation by the leaders of the campaign of 1896 that it was to be one of political education. Its managers on both sides professed to place their dependence for success upon a clear setting forth before the people of the questions at issue, both by speakers and by printed matter, exclusive of the customary support of party journals. More than any recent campaign, it was one of instruction by oral address. It was a method demanded by a desperate emergency.

In a volume mentioned upon the title-page of this book the writer ventured the statement that one of the chief factors in the settlement of political problems in the future will be the power of instructive, reasonable, and persuasive speech, and that the distance is not far to a restored oratory, and a revived eloquence which shall be needed again as they have been employed in the past and that men will turn to hear what their leaders will have to tell them, —" and leadership may depend largely upon the manner of the telling." Some months after, the last remark was illustrated in a political convention held in Chicago. Viewed simply as an oratorical triumph, it may be asserted that notwithstanding all that has been said about it by those who were not present or by those who were—after their enthusiasm had cooled—the fact still remains that when a subject, an occasion, and what antiquity called " a speaking man " conspire to a single purpose, the multitude must follow their leading. To be sure, the atmosphere may be charged with contagious and responsive sentiment and emotion, and the wayward currents of opinion may be setting in the same general direction, but it is a magnetic centre to which they converge, itself giving off and receiving back an effluence of power to the admiration and amazement of all beholders. There are plenty of reasons why such a concurrence of forces and favorable conditions may not often occur. Great occasions and crises cannot be arranged for like a pyrotechnic display. Auroral lights are not provided to order by the weather bureau. But when all elements happen to be in true conjunction, and the unexpected word is spoken, men recognize and obey a power greater than the multitude because multiplied by its numbers. They may afterwards laugh at their submission, as they ridicule their timidity after the tempest has blown over, but the fact remains and has become a part of their personal experience. The history of oratory has preserved the record of such episodes, warranting the supposition that there will be more of them in the future.   If so, there may be a revival of that form of instruction and persuasion which has counted for the most in stirring times.   It is the same as at Athens in the fifth century before our era, and at Rome in the first, in crusading Europe in the middle ages, in France in the seventeenth century, in England in the eighteenth, and in America in the nineteenth.   Eloquence will have its depressions and may be silent for years and generations; but when a cause becomes so vital that men can no longer keep silence the prophets will appear from unlooked for quarters, and the nation will listen to their message with more immediate and profound interest than to any other manner of revelation.

VI.

AFTER-DINNER REMARKS.

THIS form of the occasional address is by no means modern in its origin. Readers of Homer will recall Argive feasts after which there was much speaking, with a definite purpose in view. Indeed it is some- The antiquity times difficult to determine then as of the custom. now whether the eating or the speaking was the principal feature of the occasion. The order, however, has always remained the same, and to reverse it would probably be fatal to the total result, however much the speeches might be improved. For with nature's abhorrence of two such important processes as assimilation of food and production of thought being carried on simultaneously a compromise is likely to follow. Either the dinner or the speech will suffer, and sometimes both. In any case " re-

marks '' are not made under the most favorable
conditions, nor is dining the unalloyed pleasure
it might be were there no speech to be made.
Of course this does not apply to the rambling
talk into which a person may be unexpectedly
betrayed at the last moment under the generous influence of meats and drinks; for this
after-dinner speaking is very comprehensive,
and may include the depth of foolishness and
the height of wisdom. What is contemplated
here, is the speech for a purpose, which the
guest knows he is to be called upon to make,
and of which he has had timely warning. As
such it is not the easiest oratorical task. To
note some of the difficulties and dangers of it
will serve to make plain certain needs of the
speaker.

To the inexperienced there is likely to arise
the dangerous hope that the occasion itself will
The occasion furnishing material. furnish material for remarks; or that
other speakers will suggest trains of
thought which can be seized upon as
the flow of soul becomes full and strong.
Even an adroit restatement of the commonplaces of the hour is not impossible, and is far

better than the appearance of labor in preparation. Such suggestions should be received as the whisperings of laziness and procrastination. The commonplaces of the occasion belong to the presiding officer as his privilege and duty in his introductory remarks; and as for the suggestions of others, they usually pursue the exhaustive method rather than the suggestive, and make the most of what unused ideas remain to them. Add to this the difficulty with which cogitations, worth uttering, are pursued amidst entertaining speech and laughter and comment right and left, to say nothing of tobacco smoke and the effervescence of champagne—if it is that sort of a dinner. If it is a cold lunch there are other impediments to mental activity and creative thought.

He is not, therefore, a wise man who comes to the feast with no oil for his lamp. He will find that others have brought no Prevision and more than they will be likely to need forethought. for themselves as the hours wear on toward midnight or morning. For what is the real nature of such an occasion but an intellectual tourney disguised, which the uninitiated are

21

apt to take for a post-prandial conversation entirely informal. Suppose it were; how few can shine in these days which have forgotten Coleridge and Wilson and the famous monologists of their time. Their art of monopolizing table-talk is a lost one, and this is a still higher art in which some of those ancient worthies would make a sorry figure if called upon to stand up and address the crowd after a dozen other wits had improved their chance. The invited " orator of the day " who has the occasion all to himself has an unharvested **Preparation and gleaning.** field before him, with no one to point out what he has left untouched. But the late speaker at a dinner follows a dozen others, a very gleaner, while before the company he must be a competitor for the prize of their attention and applause. Such an occasion comes nearer than any other to the literary contests of Olympia. Not with the seriousness and stateliness of its poetic, dramatic, and oratorical competitions; but in the swift succession of speakers, in the interest to be kept up, in the added difficulty of improvisation, in reference and retort there is often a tournament worthy the best intellects in the best ages. Therefore, if any difficulties and embarrassments can be forestalled by judicious prevision of what is likely to be said, and of what should be said, these ought to be anticipated. Above all a wide and comprehensive survey of the entire range of topics pertinent to the occasion will save a speaker from the feeling that he has been defrauded, which is likely to creep over him as he hears one after another of his points taken up by previous speakers. A large shrinkage must be allowed for in the fullest preparation, unless one has an early position or an assigned topic. In this case there will be still less excuse for its indifferent treatment.

Here arises another danger, that of over-preparation. It is one of the real difficulties of this kind of address that even weighty subjects must be treated in lighter vein. Not every one can do this successfully. To draw the line between lightness and levity is as hard as to distinguish between sobriety and dulness. Accordingly, many a man who can write a treatise cannot discuss his favorite theme to the edification of a company indisposed to mental exertion. All the more necessity will there be for such preparation as will comport with the spirit of the occasion, and the intellectual condition of his hearers.   The speaker is to remember that it is not a meeting of scientists, philologists, bankers, or politicians in their professional capacity. Whatever he says is to be made interesting and easy of apprehension.   Neither his subject nor himself is to be a bore.

This suggests two directions which will bear stating: first, the prime qualification of an after-dinner speaker is that he be entertaining.   The form of his speech may be instructive, reminiscent, or hortatory, but in spirit it must be interesting.   The audience is proverbially good-natured, for the best of reasons. It is also patient—at first; but it has a right to be entertained and even amused, or else to hoard its fleeting moments for the use of those who are able to interest it.   There are several ways in which a speaker can be interesting, but perhaps the chief of these is by a judicious use of the good story.   It is not every speaker who has an anecdote to relate, nor every other who can relate one well. A plentifully stocked memory and effective narration commonly go together. When these are combined with a third faculty—the sense of fitness—anecdote becomes a prominent element in the speech that brings down the house. Indeed the house is sometimes kept at the roaring point by a succession of narratives, the application of which it is not always easy to discover. The table has been listening to " Iagoo, marvellous story-teller," and has mistaken a string of mirth-provoking accounts for a good speech. Therein the speaker also has made a mistake ; but the audience is forgiving in this direction because it has been amused. But when anecdotes are pat, not too numerous, and illustrating sound sense, two principal constituents of an after-dinner speech are present.

There is one other—brevity. Not every speaker can be wise or witty, but all can practise that virtue which is the soul of wit. Hearers will excuse dulness, *Brevity desirable.* and even erudition, in speeches if they are brief. But speakers are the worst of timekeepers.   Between their fear lest they betray poverty of thought, and anxiety lest they shall not finish what they have to say, the much-enduring company suffers many things from prolix talkers.   It is not an unknown occurrence that such an one has been vociferously applauded to drown him and " down " him; when, alas, he mistook the purpose of the cheers and stamping, and thought he must continue to be entertaining.   The only remedy is the five- or ten-minute rule of the remorseless gavel.   Most speakers are better pleased to be knocked down than to descend with grace, or to collapse before they think their time has expired.

A good post-prandial speech is therefore no trifling matter, nor a matter to be trifled with. **Requisites of preparation.** The general rather than the minute preparation, the extensive rather than the intensive or exhaustive treatment, the abundant rather than the profound resources and material, and the art to omit and supply upon need, and above all to illuminate and adorn with appropriate and illustrative anecdote, are the chief essentials to success.   The reward of it will be evident and speedily forth-coming. Never is an audience more uncritical and responsive. Applause is free and unrestrained, and if it do not throw the speaker off his centre, is helpful and encouraging. He will, nevertheless, need all his discipline as an extemporaneous speaker to carry himself creditably, treating his topic in proper proportion, in manner appropriate to the occasion, and with reasonable brevity. After he has done his best he will say with Lowell, returning from a feast (and as Goethe said before him), " I made the best speech of my life to-night—in the carriage as I was coming home, saying over to myself the things I ought to have said, but forgot to say, to the company."

If the reader wishes to see what a place the after-dinner speech occupies in literature he may begin with the *Iliad* and *Odys-* sey; but he will find an abundance of it in the works of our American orators. Their lighter " Remarks " and "Addresses " are interspersed with weightier utterances in volume after volume. Brief and ephemeral as many of them were, these lesser

The literature of the after-dinner speech.

productions have been deemed worthy of a
place among the best orations of Webster,
Everett, Choate, Winthrop, Phillips, Sumner,
and Curtis; while among the publications of
scholars and statesmen still living are similar
proofs of versatility and talent.   These occupy
a place in the literature of the occasional address that can be filled by no other form of it,
and have their own value in illustrating the history that was making in the times of their delivery.   To it they give a living reality as of
things occurring daily, as viewed by contemporaries, and as commented upon in the freedom of good fellowship.

The custom is an old one, but likely to survive; and the educated man therefore cannot
afford to neglect any means which will assist
him in this form of occasional address.   Many
a noble enterprise has been started at the fes-
Value of such tive board by men who knew when
opportunities. their fellows were in a mood to take
large and benevolent views of affairs, and many
a just tribute has there been paid to worth, and
many a good impulse given to honorable living
and earnest endeavor.   In some respects it

presents a most favorable opportunity for a speaker effectually to address his fellow-men. There is much to gain in silver speech by one who is equal to the occasion. There are also compensations in golden silence for those who, uncalled and undisturbed, are permitted to listen to the wisdom and the wit of after-dinner speakers.

A backward glance over the general subject of the Occasional Address in its three divisions of Structure, Qualities, and Forms, reveals much that is common to it and the kindred topics of judicial, deliberative, and homiletic discourse. Much, too, is revealed of still other forms of composition, thoughts, and diction; their ordering, and the qualities which make them most effective are the properties of every kind of writing, to be distributed according to its class and purpose. But more than any other, demonstrative oratory deals with the understandings of all men as related to their sensibilities, their affections, and their emotions. The men who have lived lives worth recounting, the events in which human effort has culminated, the present truth which needs enforcing, the studies of the scholar, the science of government, the interchange of kindly feeling, and the promptings of generous sentiment, all these in their manifold phases belong to the sphere of demonstrative speech. It shows forth the worth of virtues, and the significance of occurrences, which otherwise might be passed by unheeded. It records and publishes chapters in the history which is fluid or growing solid; and it connects present events with past causes and future consequences.   It is the historian, the instructor, and the prophet of all the people irrespective of caste, creed, or party.   Free to all who will listen, it is itself the child of freedom, possible only where speech is untrammelled and criticism given without fear and received without resentment.

Nor can the speaker hide behind the screen of impersonality and give out his utterances from mysterious retreats.   Like the legislators of old who proposed laws with halters about their necks, the occasional orator carries into open day his personal responsibility for what he says. His judges are the people, who will not be bribed by flattery as they will not mob him for telling them their faults. If he stand by the truth they will in turn stand by him, and his power will be redoubled by their allegiance. Therefore his opportunity and his reward are great; the one too rare to be neglected, the other too abundant to be despised. It is worth the study and labor of years to do what some have accomplished in this field. Their names are landmarks in the literature and history of eloquence, an honor to their own age and an inspiration to the future.

THE END

INDEX

A

W